OFFICERS and SOLDIERS of

THE AMERICAN CIVIL WAR

(THE WAR OF SECESSION)

Volume Two
Cavalry and Artillery

André JOUINEAU
and Jean-Marie MONGIN
Translated from the French by Alan McKAY

HISTOIRE & COLLECTIONS

THE AMERIC

Operations during the American Civil War were dictated mainly by geography: the Eastern half of the United States is divided into two quite distinct regions by the Appalachians. To the east are the most populated states, the main rail and road infrastructures and the capitals of the two belligerents, only 95 miles apart. To the west in those days, the land was wilder, under-developed and lightly populated. The principal operations took place in the east, where a successful operation could be decisive for the outcome of the war.

From 1861, the Anaconda Plan, prepared by General Scott, fixed the Union's objectives: blockading the Confederation's ports in order to stifle its economy which depended greatly on foreign trade; and controlling the Mississippi in order to split the Southern states in two. But this was not enough for public opinion: it wanted action; it soon became clear that this would be necessary because, for as long as the South had an army, it would refuse to surrender. Faced with this stubborn resistance, the Union had to modify its strategy: the Confederation's territory would have to be occupied in order to deprive it of its industrial and agricultural ressources, and its potential for human recruitment.

As the country was particularly hostile to northern troops, more than a third of the Army was immobilised in garrisons covering the 520 000 sq. kms which had been occupied by 1863. Realising that they did not have enough men to keep order, in 1864 the northern generals preferred a strategy using raids, conducted by whole armies and intended to destroy the South's means of supply, in particular its rail infrastructure. The first raid was carried out by General Sherman who made his 60 000-strong army cover the 250 miles separating Atlanta from Savannah.

From the outset the South adopted a defensive strategy. It did not have to defeat anybody in order to win the war, it had either to discourage the North by showing them that they had neither the human nor the material means to avoid the southern states seceding; or to gain enough time for England or France to decide upon official recognition. Even when Lee invaded the North in 1862 and again in 1863, his objectives were limited: rallying the states that were presumed to be favourable to the ideas of the South, renewing supplies, and capturing a big town in order to have a bargaining counter should negotiations become necessary.

At the beginning of the conflict, President Davis wanted to imitate Washington: retreating in the face of stronger armies, attacking weaker ones and avoiding big battles in order not to risk squandering the South's army, which was the only true guarantor of the Confederation's independence. But he had to contend with the Governors of the States and the population, who both wanted troops to be present to defend their own territories, and with the fiery southern temperament, which was much keener on attack.

A strategy of defence by means of attack started to emerge during the campaigns: the Confederation's territory was defended by using the internal lines of communication, in order to concentrate dispersed forces rapidly against the northern invaders; and when the opportunity presented itself, the southern armies could push home their advantage by going over to the offensive.

General Jackson showed his perfect mastery of these internal lines during his campaign along the Shenandoah Valley in 1862 where, outnumbered three to one, he held against the dispersed Union divisions by hitting them one by one and then going to rejoin Lee's army to the south-east of Richmond by train.

Logistics hindered the movement of the armies and confined operational plans. In fact, vast portions of territory were very sparsely populated and those that were cultivated were rapidly devastated by the passage of the troops; this prevented the troops from living off the land. They became dependent on supplies, transported in wagons which followed them and slowed them down considerably. The operational lines were often limited to the watercourses and railways which were the fastest means of transporting supplies. The South used cavalry and guerilla raids to try to make the powerful armies from the North retreat by disrupting their logistics system.

When war burst out, the senior officers had very little theoretical strategy. Indeed the lessons at West Point, which they all attended, insisted particularly on mathematics, fortifications, administration and tactics. Only Jomini's principles were touched upon, and not much notice was taken of him: Grant himself admitted never having read him. Moreover garrison life and a few fights against the Indians did not exactly encourage the study of strategy.

The only experience of conventional warfare that American generals had had, was the Mexican War of 1846-48, which did reveal however their liking for audacious manoeuvres and their capacity for initiative.

During the Civil War, the conduct of operations showed that the generals could master a Napoleonic style of war, but could also take advantage of new technologies like the telegraph and the railways, which enabled them to control and carry out vast movements, and to concentrate dispersed army corps rapidly. One of their favourite manoeuvres during the conflict was a turning movement like those in the Battles of Ulm and Marengo, but it nearly always failed because, unlike Napoleon's opponents, this enemy was just as mobile.

These movements were sometimes bigger than those of the Napoleonic period. In order to avoid presenting too compact a target, the armies advanced in a much more extended front line; the armies also formed up much further away from the enemy. The attacker had therefore to cover a greater distance in the firing area, and the fighting was almost exclusively a shooting match between infantrymen, bayonet attacks being used only as a menace to dislodge those who had less morale. Battles were therefore longer and less decisive. Finally, defence was now stronger than attack, especially with the increased use of trenches.

The belligerents did not learn any lessons from the Crimean War (1853-1856) which had shown what effect rifled guns could have on masses of men in serried ranks. They kept using obsolete assault formations, conceived for bayonet attacks and not very practical against the infantry's new firepower.

At the beginning of the war, the American generals kept up the offensive spirit which had been successful during the Mexican War and tried to apply the old Napoleonic tactics of infantry assaults covered by artillery. But artillery pieces had not progressed technically as fast as rifles. The range of the artillery was now inadequate in preparing the infantry's advance.

In order to avoid concentrating too many soldiers in the firing area, the assault was carried through in succesive waves at intervals of 50 to 300 yards, most often 150. If the officers managed to keep control, the adversary would be hit by successive fresh units and pushed back before having time to use his reserves. But in reality, since the first line of attack was usually delayed by the terrain or by the enemy, the

AN CIVIL WAR

units of the following waves used to get muddled up and formed only a confused mass of men. The Confederates experienced this at Shiloh where, having deployed their troops in ranks, the generals gradually lost control of the troops, obliging them to reorganise their command structure, right in the middle of the battle.

A general in command of a division did not usually put all his brigades into the line, he kept a column in reserve. Passing the reserves through the front line was a dangerous manoeuvre and could lead to confusion. When units in the front line were too serried, they would lie down enabling the reserve line to pass through; at Petersburg (1864), the enthusiastic recruits of the 1st Maine charged over the veterans who had thrown themselves to the ground for protection.

Well before the Europeans, the Americans discovered the much more modern technique of moving up in leaps and bounds; whilst attacking Fort Donelson in 1862, the Northern units threw themselves to the ground when the firing from the other side became too intense, before getting up and resuming the assault. From Spring 1864 onwards, the Union used large columns in an attempt to break the enemy's positions situated in wooded terrain because Grant was determined to destroy the Army of Virginia at all costs. In fact the deployment of infantry units during an attack differed according to the brigade, division or corps commander's tactical principles.

In 1863 at Fredericksburg, General Newton drew up his troops in mixed order: a brigade in line with a regiment up front in skirmishing position, flanked on either side by a brigade whose regiments were drawn up in columns by division.

In May 1864, at Spotssylvania the 20 000 men of Hancock's 2nd Corps attacked the Confederate positions in closed ranks because the generals had learnt that the artillery had been removed from the objective: the 2nd division regiments were in columns by division, the 3rd were deployed in two lines and the 1rst formed a massive 40-rank-deep column of soldiers who had been obliged to remove the percussion caps from their rifles and fix bayonets!

From the Battle of Antietam (September 1862) onwards, the armies used more and more elaborate field fortifications to protect themselves. In three days they could build a parapet with cleared ground in the front and protected batteries at the rear. With more time, trenches stayed with logs, reinforced with sandbags or gabions filled with earth, and shell-proof shelters could be dug and built. Mines made from shells with percussion detonators were used for the first time at Williamsburg in 1862.

Larger mines were used to attack fortifications: these were explosives which were placed under the enemy positions, using underground passages. The mine which exploded at Petersburg (1864) created a crater 150 feet across, 60 feet long and 30 feet deep, burying a whole confederate regiment and battery under the debris.

The Cavalry

The cavalry was rarely used *en masse* on the battlefield except towards the end of the war by General Sheridan, during his Shenandoah Valley Campaign, in 1864. It usually fought dismounted; most cavalry charges were sacrificial actions, used to gain time when covering a retreat or bringing up re-inforcements. Cavalrymen were used especially as scouts to protect their army's advance and discover the intentions of the ennemy. The theatre of operations was so spread out that the cavalry was able to carry out raids on the enemy's rear in order to cut his lines of communication; in 1862, Stuart's cavalry went round the Army of the Potomac — 100 miles — in four days.

For charging, the Union cavalry used the the sabre because of its psychological effect: it frightened the enemy and encouraged the user to make contact. The Confederates preferred the revolver, less chivalrous, but just as effective. Faced with the infantry's firepower, the cavalry however normally fought dismounted.

The regiment was then deployed in loose or skirmishing order, with one or two mounted squadrons held back in support; a quarter of the men was left to guard the horses, an eighth only when the horses were tethered. In the first part of the war, the Confederate cavalry, recruited among rich men used to riding, was superior to its northern counterpart which, since it was not at all properly appreciated by its own army, was often relegated to escort and mail duties.

The Artillery

The artillery included some of the most professional men in the army, because of the technical demands of their arm. An artillery limber team could unhitch and fire a cannon within 30 seconds and hitch up in one minute, a whole battery took three times as much time to carry out the same manoeuvres. Each cannon had about 100 shots, of which three-quarters were full shells, the rest explosive shells and grapeshot. In one hour a battery could run out of ammunition if it fired non-stop.

At Gettysburg, General Hunt, commanding the artillery of the Army of the Potomac, complained that his artillerymen fired as quickly as possible, i.e. three shots a minute, in order to run out of ammunition and therefore to be able to retire from the front. He explained that a rate of one shot a minute was best for shooting accurately and not wasting ammunition. The batteries tried to set themselves up just over the crest of a hill to protect themselves from enemy shots. Artillery was of little use in attack because the defenders were always sheltered and it could not get in close because of the range of rifled weapons; however in defence, it was particularly effective with grapeshot and could therefore be used *en masse*, without infantry support, like at Gettysburg where 25 northern cannon held the front along Plum Run. It was also used in reserve to plug breaches made in the front line by the attackers. The Confederates, whose weapons were often of lesser quality, did not often shoot against other batteries, preferring to keep their ammunition for the enemy infantry.

The Civil War was the most murderous war in the history of the United States, totalling more dead than all the wars fought by the Americans up to Viet Nam. The North lost about 360 000 men and the Confederates at least 260 000, to which have to be added the deaths due to privation amongst the civilian population in the South.

Finally, in spite of numerous European observers, the European armies learnt no lessons from the conflict. On this side of the Atlantic, infantry tactics remained obsolete until the Bœr War, and even until the First World War.

Study by Dominique Sanches

THE UNION CAVALRY

At the beginning of the conflict the Union Cavalry was made up of five regular cavalry regiments going back to the first decade of the century. Each sub-division originally had very precise tasks. On the eve of the Civil War, the United States Cavalry consisted of:
- 2 regiments of Dragoons
- 1 regiment of mounted infantry
- 2 regiments of cavalry.

A third cavalry regiment was constituted in May 1861.

After the First battle of Bull Run, Congress authorised President Lincoln to accept the service of 31 regiments of volunteers for as long as the war lasted.

In August 1861, the dragoon, riflemen and cavalry regiments were regrouped into the same arm and numbered 1 to 5 according to the date of their creation. Daffodil yellow became the only distinctive colour for the cavalry.

After July 1863, the War Department set up a cavalry office with responsibility for supplies, equipment and horses, taking over from the Quartermaster's Department.

The cavalry rapidly increased its numbers and although it was of less value than its Southern equivalent, it managed to acquit itself well against the enemy.

During the last two years of the conflict however, it greatly contributed to General Lee's defeat. It became a terribly efficient weapon because it had overwhelming numbers, mobility and power, and it was used properly.

When hostilities ceased, there were 272 cavalry units in the Northern Army.

THE REGULAR CAVALRY REGIMENT

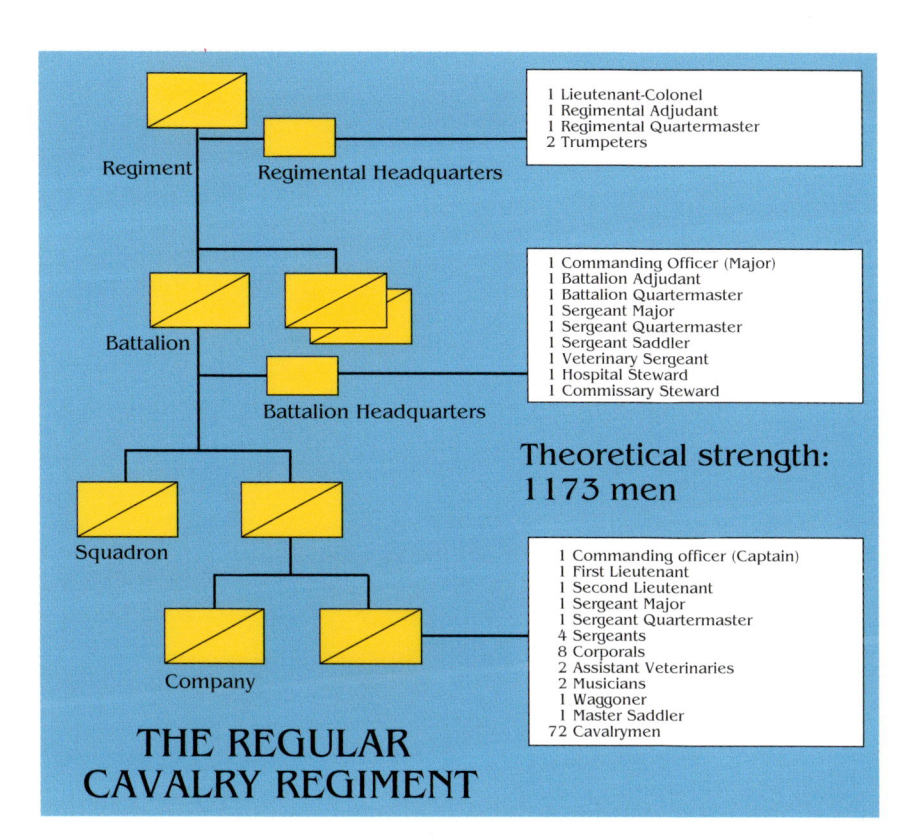

Regimental Headquarters
- 1 Lieutenant-Colonel
- 1 Regimental Adjudant
- 1 Regimental Quartermaster
- 2 Trumpeters

Battalion Headquarters
- 1 Commanding Officer (Major)
- 1 Battalion Adjudant
- 1 Battalion Quartermaster
- 1 Sergeant Major
- 1 Sergeant Quartermaster
- 1 Sergeant Saddler
- 1 Veterinary Sergeant
- 1 Hospital Steward
- 1 Commissary Steward

Theoretical strength: 1173 men

Company
- 1 Commanding officer (Captain)
- 1 First Lieutenant
- 1 Second Lieutenant
- 1 Sergeant Major
- 1 Sergeant Quartermaster
- 4 Sergeants
- 8 Corporals
- 2 Assistant Veterinaries
- 2 Musicians
- 1 Waggoner
- 1 Master Saddler
- 72 Cavalrymen

THE VOLUNTEER CAVALRY REGIMENT

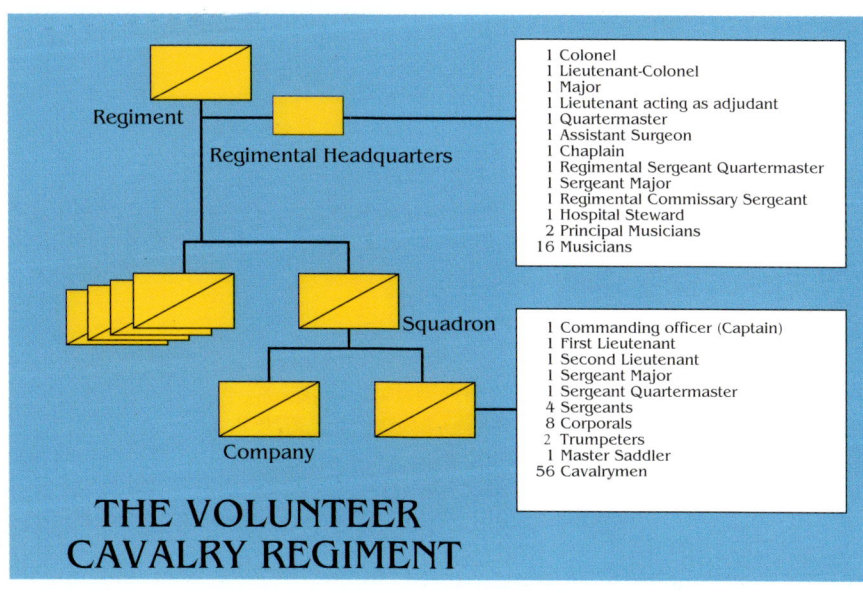

Regimental Headquarters
- 1 Colonel
- 1 Lieutenant-Colonel
- 1 Major
- 1 Lieutenant acting as adjudant
- 1 Quartermaster
- 1 Assistant Surgeon
- 1 Chaplain
- 1 Regimental Sergeant Quartermaster
- 1 Sergeant Major
- 1 Regimental Commissary Sergeant
- 1 Hospital Steward
- 2 Principal Musicians
- 16 Musicians

Company
- 1 Commanding officer (Captain)
- 1 First Lieutenant
- 1 Second Lieutenant
- 1 Sergeant Major
- 1 Sergeant Quartermaster
- 4 Sergeants
- 8 Corporals
- 2 Trumpeters
- 1 Master Saddler
- 56 Cavalrymen

A CAVALRY REGIMENT

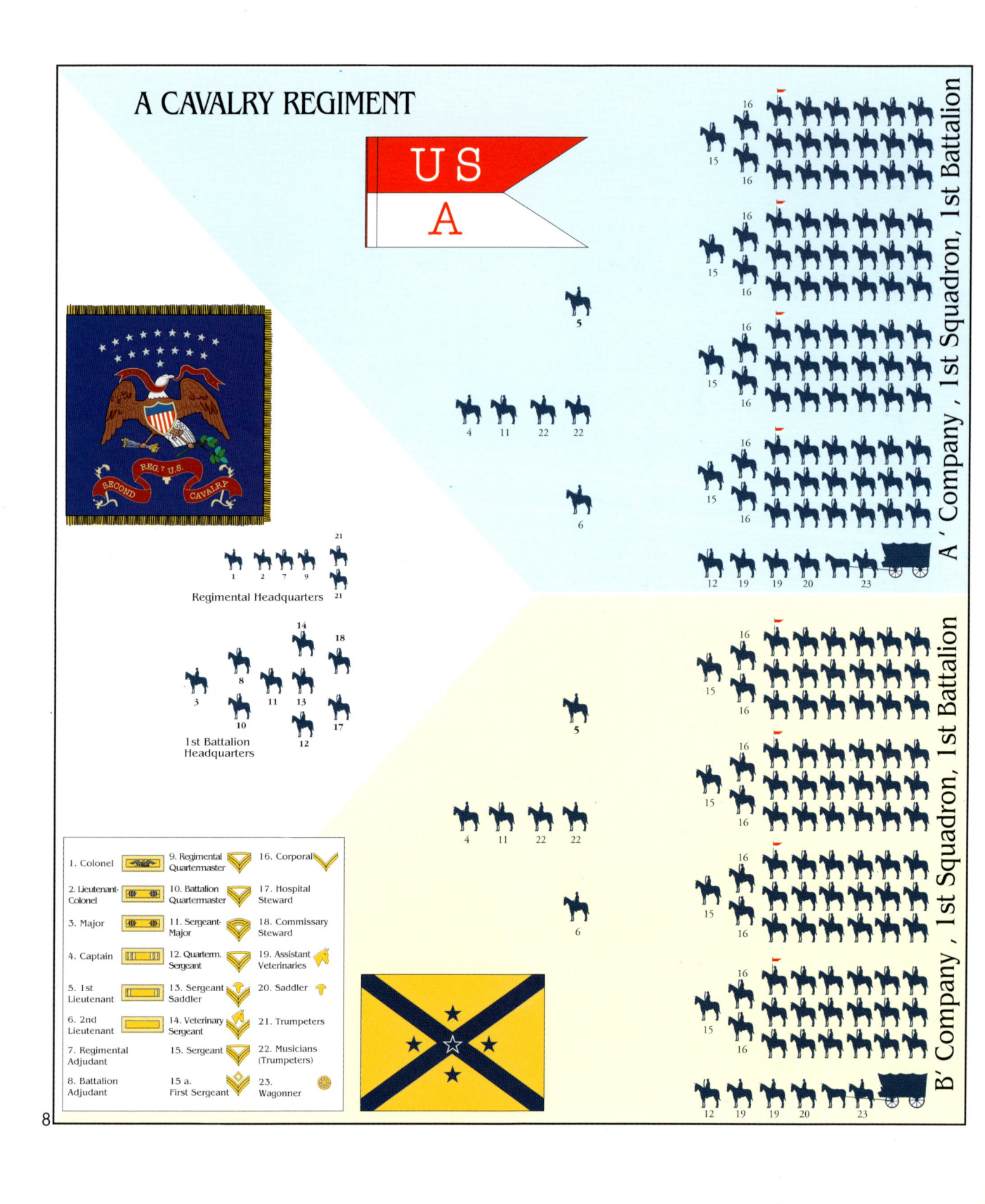

Regimental Headquarters
1. 2. 7. 9. 21. 21.

1st Battalion Headquarters
3. 8. 14. 18. 10. 11. 13. 17. 12.

A' Company, 1st Squadron, 1st Battalion

B' Company, 1st Squadron, 1st Battalion

1. Colonel	9. Regimental Quartermaster	16. Corporal
2. Lieutenant-Colonel	10. Battalion Quartermaster	17. Hospital Steward
3. Major	11. Sergeant-Major	18. Commissary Steward
4. Captain	12. Quarterm. Sergeant	19. Assistant Veterinaries
5. 1st Lieutenant	13. Sergeant Saddler	20. Saddler
6. 2nd Lieutenant	14. Veterinary Sergeant	21. Trumpeters
7. Regimental Adjutant	15. Sergeant	22. Musicians (Trumpeters)
8. Battalion Adjutant	15 a. First Sergeant	23. Wagonner

The UNION CAVALRYMAN

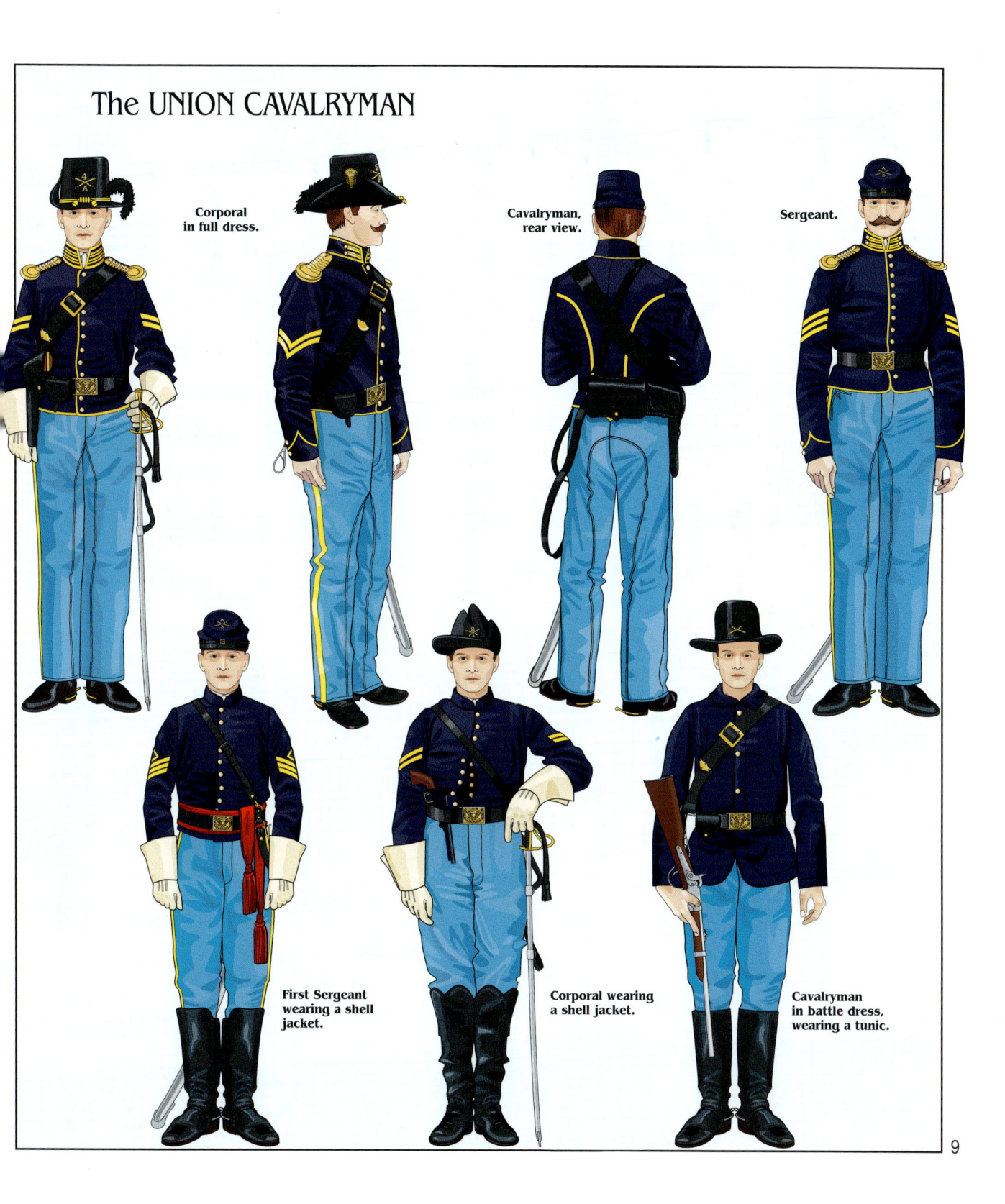

Corporal in full dress.

Cavalryman, rear view.

Sergeant.

First Sergeant wearing a shell jacket.

Corporal wearing a shell jacket.

Cavalryman in battle dress, wearing a tunic.

The UNION CAVALRYMAN

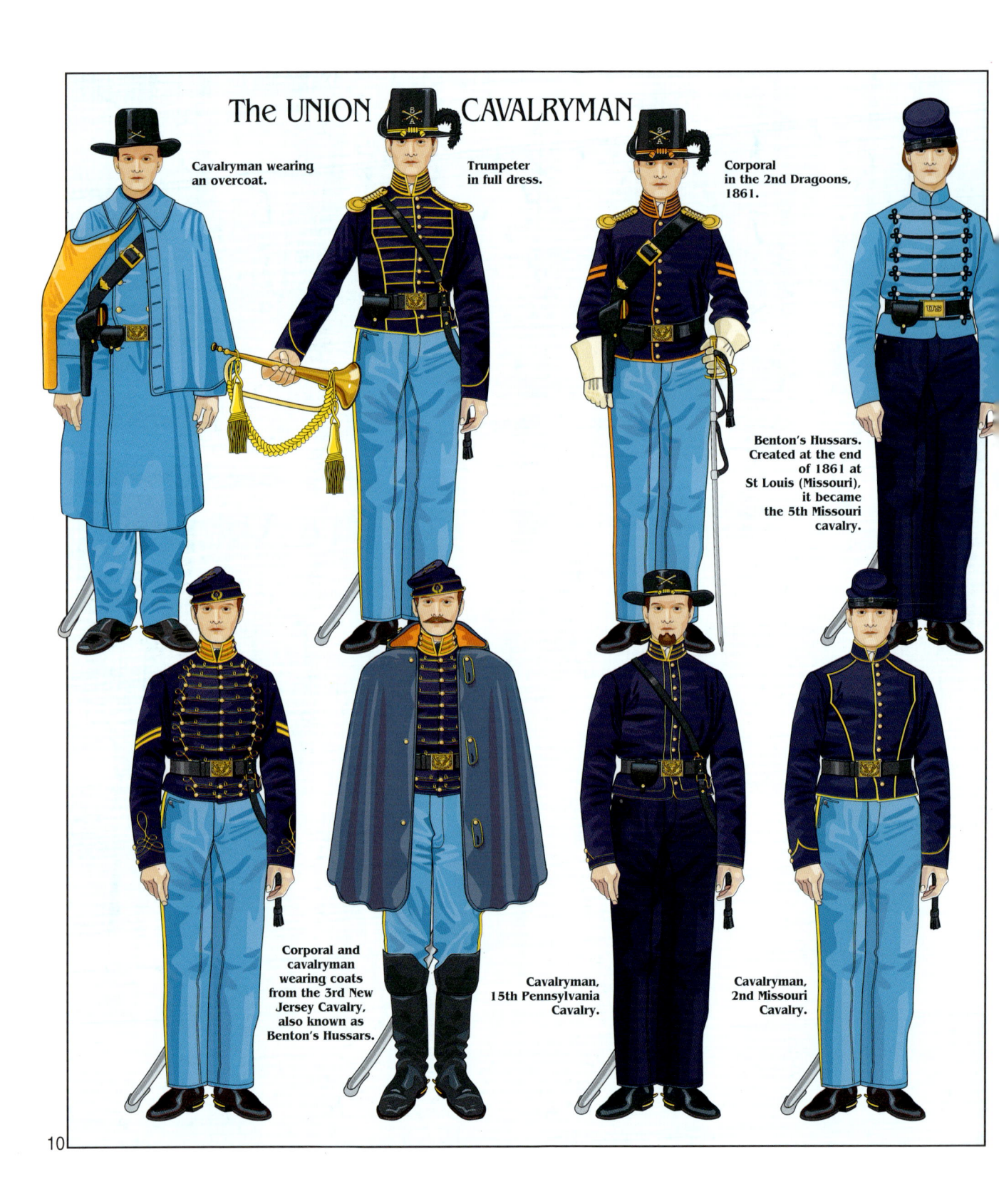

Cavalryman wearing an overcoat.

Trumpeter in full dress.

Corporal in the 2nd Dragoons, 1861.

Benton's Hussars. Created at the end of 1861 at St Louis (Missouri), it became the 5th Missouri cavalry.

Corporal and cavalryman wearing coats from the 3rd New Jersey Cavalry, also known as Benton's Hussars.

Cavalryman, 15th Pennsylvania Cavalry.

Cavalryman, 2nd Missouri Cavalry.

NON-COMMISSIONED OFFICERS and OTHER RANKS

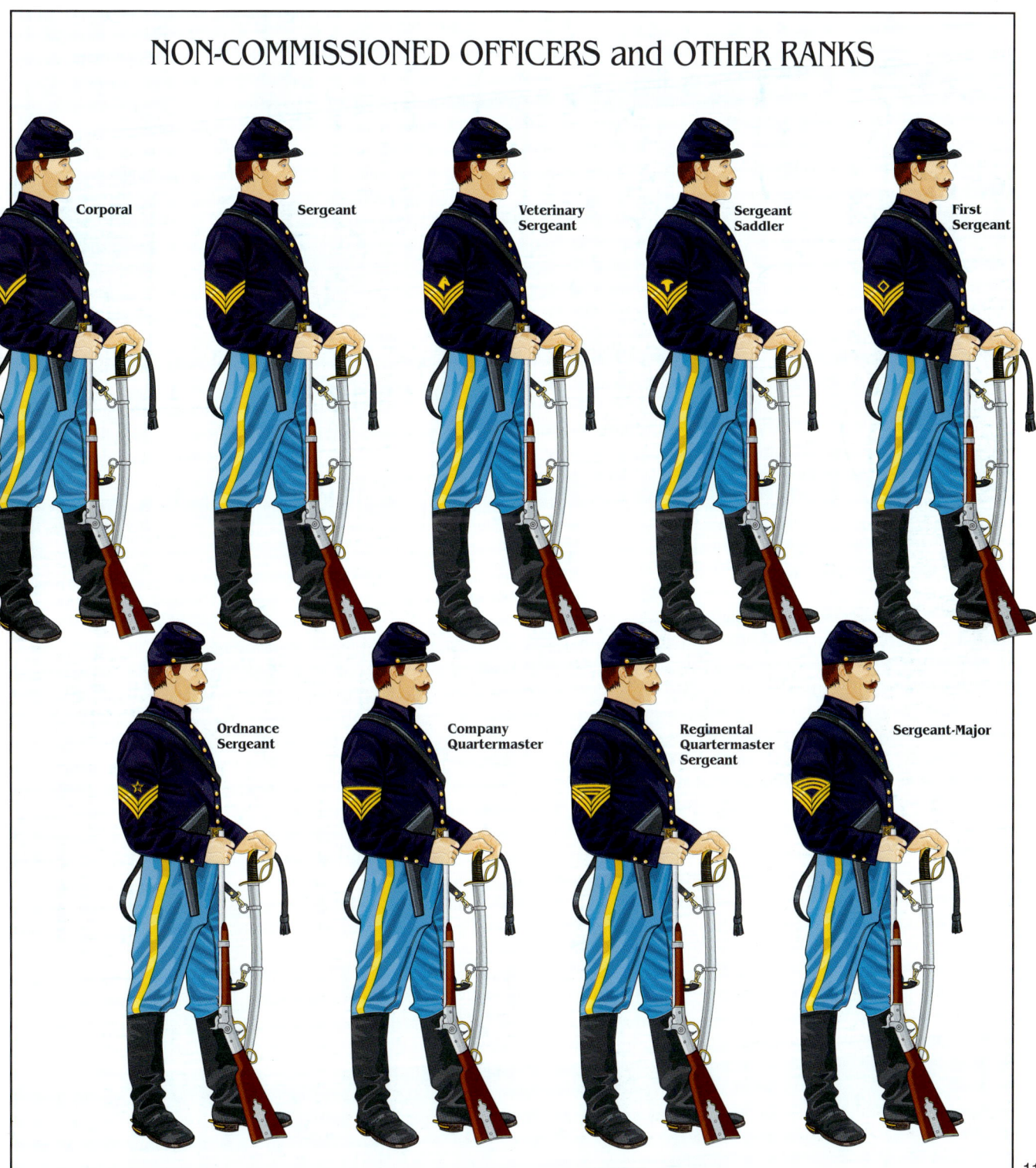

Corporal

Sergeant

Veterinary Sergeant

Sergeant Saddler

First Sergeant

Ordnance Sergeant

Company Quartermaster

Regimental Quartermaster Sergeant

Sergeant-Major

PARTS of the UNIFORM

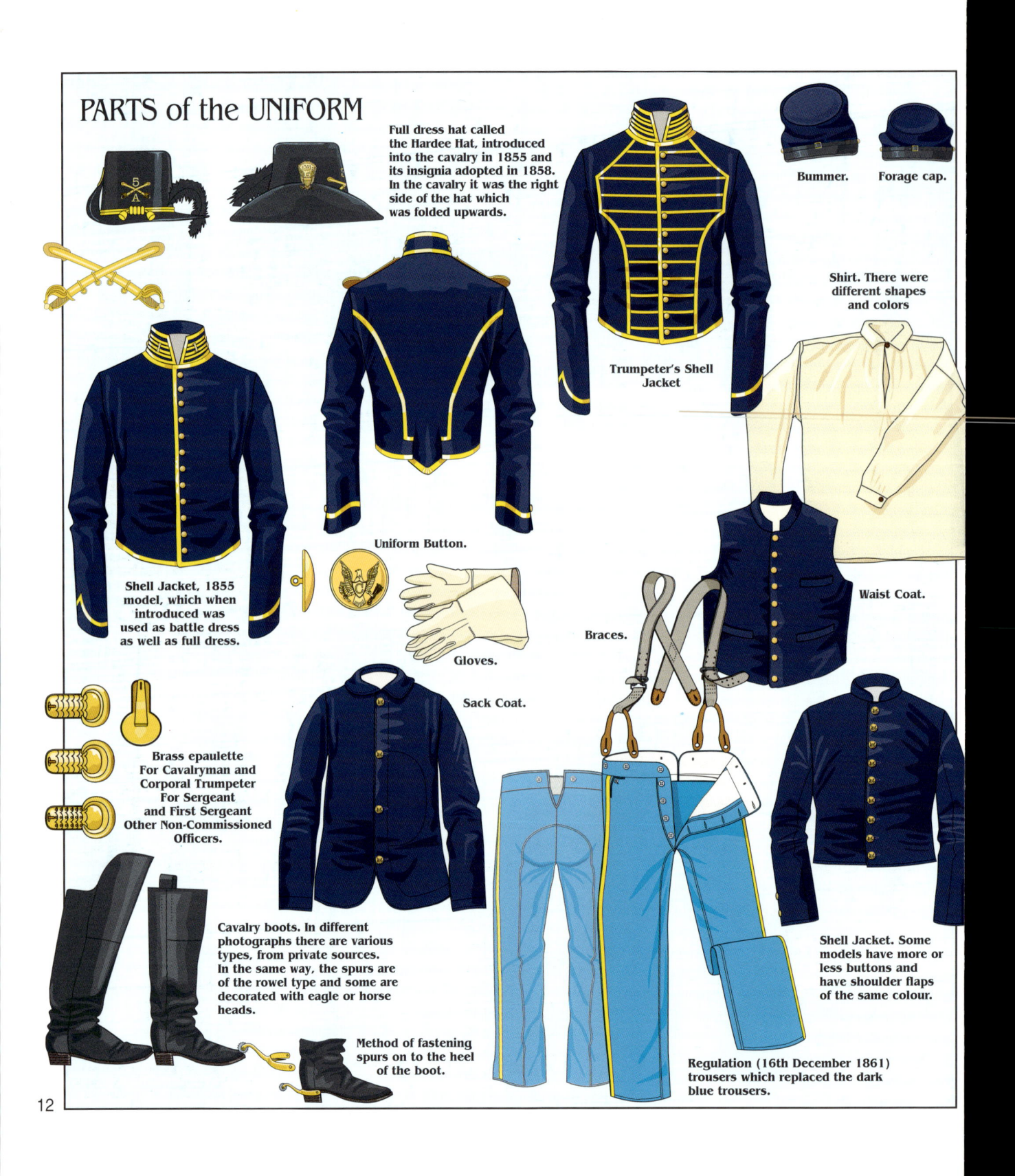

Full dress hat called the Hardee Hat, introduced into the cavalry in 1855 and its insignia adopted in 1858. In the cavalry it was the right side of the hat which was folded upwards.

Bummer.

Forage cap.

Trumpeter's Shell Jacket

Shirt. There were different shapes and colors

Shell Jacket, 1855 model, which when introduced was used as battle dress as well as full dress.

Uniform Button.

Gloves.

Braces.

Waist Coat.

Brass epaulette For Cavalryman and Corporal Trumpeter For Sergeant and First Sergeant Other Non-Commissioned Officers.

Sack Coat.

Cavalry boots. In different photographs there are various types, from private sources. In the same way, the spurs are of the rowel type and some are decorated with eagle or horse heads.

Method of fastening spurs on to the heel of the boot.

Regulation (16th December 1861) trousers which replaced the dark blue trousers.

Shell Jacket. Some models have more or less buttons and have shoulder flaps of the same colour.

12

EQUIPMENT

Although the equipment was simple and rudimentary, it was essential for the cavalryman to have a lot of firepower.

Navy Colt, .36 calibre, 1851 model.

Colt, .44 calibre, 1860 model.

Cap pouch, infantry model.

Cavalryman's equipment, Sabre, 1861 model.

Springfield carbine pistol, 1855 model.

Sharp Percussion rifle, .52 calibre, 1852 model.

Perry percussion rifle.

Cartridge pouch for the revolver and the rifle. The front pocket contains equipment for weapon maintenance.

Spencer Rifle with its loading system, with cartridge box, worn slung over the shoulder and fastened to the belt.

Bandolier with Rifle pouch.

A water flask covered with blue cloth. Models exist made out of wood or metal; some are rectangular.

SADDLERY

Corporal from "Rush's Lancers" named after its Colonel, Richard Rush, 6th Pennsylvania Cavalry. Although a lance was standard equipment, these were not used against the South's firearms.

Corporal in full dress, sitting on a Grimsley saddle.

MacClellan-type, 1859 model, head harness.

An unequipped McClellan saddle, with the rifle holder, the stirrups.

Bellyband.

MacClellan saddle, equipped with a rolled up coat and a nosebag. The saddle blanket is an 1859 model, trimmed in orange for the dragoons, yellow for the cavalry. The waterproof blanket is rolled up behind, attached with straps to the cantle. Saddlebags hang down either side.

1847 model Grimsley saddle or dragoon saddle. This saddle was created originally for the dragoons and cavalrymen. Although progressively replaced by the McClellan saddle, it remained in service throughout the whole of the Civil War.

The OFFICERS

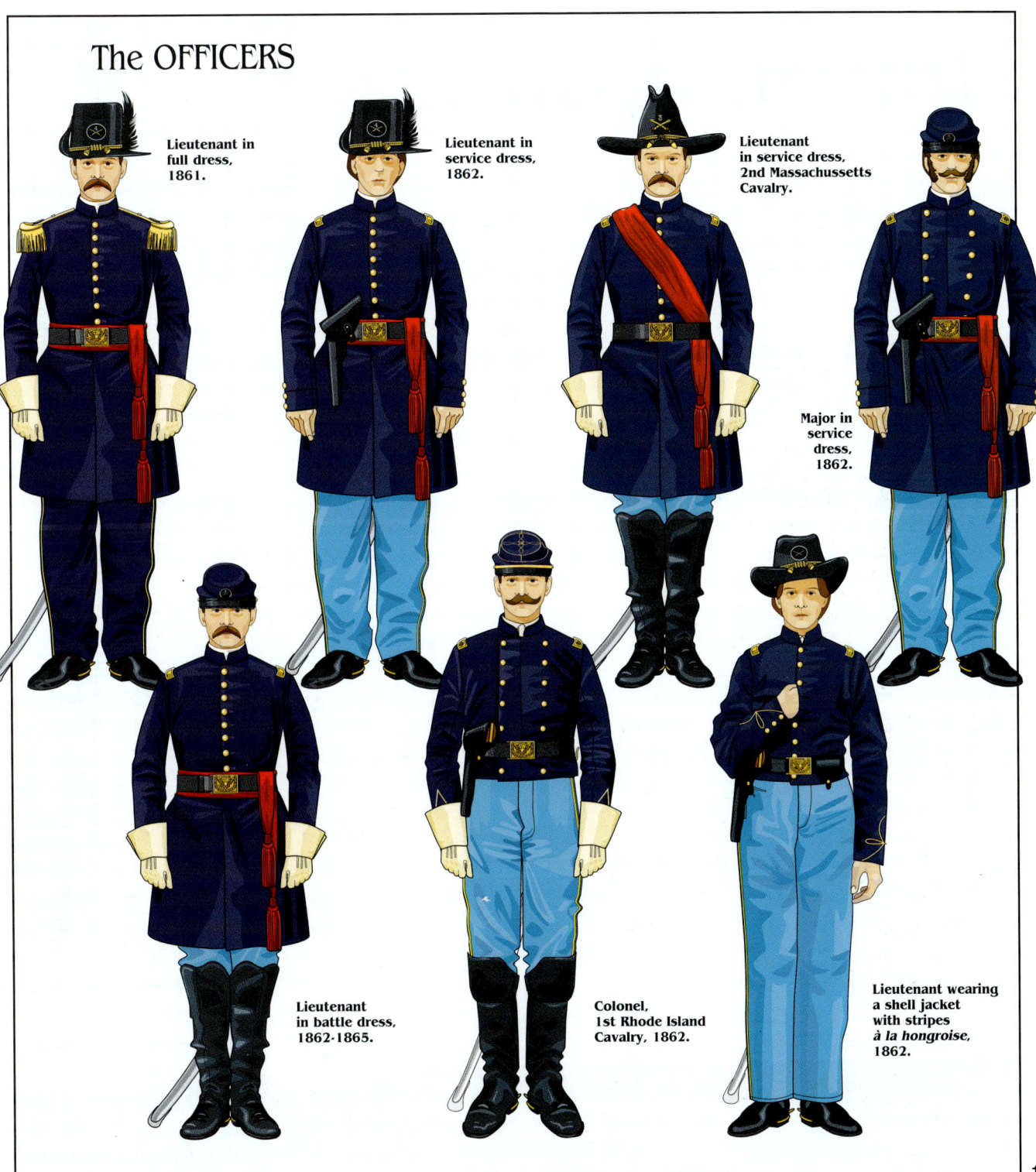

Lieutenant in full dress, 1861.

Lieutenant in service dress, 1862.

Lieutenant in service dress, 2nd Massachussetts Cavalry.

Major in service dress, 1862.

Lieutenant in battle dress, 1862-1865.

Colonel, 1st Rhode Island Cavalry, 1862.

Lieutenant wearing a shell jacket with stripes *à la hongroise*, 1862.

The OFFICERS

Lieutenant wearing an overcoat. During the war, the officers gave up wearing this coat in favour of the one worn by ordinary soldiers in order not to be an easy target for snipers.

Lieutenant in service dress, 1862.

1860 model, 44 calibre Colt.

Binoculars and their case.

Officer's equipment. The belt and the belt-plate were the same for officers and Non-Commissioned officers. The links attaching the straps to the ring of the sabre could be different, as the rear-view silhouette shows. The sabres used were 1840 or 1860 models.

Uniform button.

Cavalry gloves.

Tunic and waistcoat.

Example of an officer's boot.

Regulation trousers.

- Colonel
- Lieutenant-Colonel
- Major
- Captain
- Lieutenant
- Second-Lieutenant

The OFFICERS

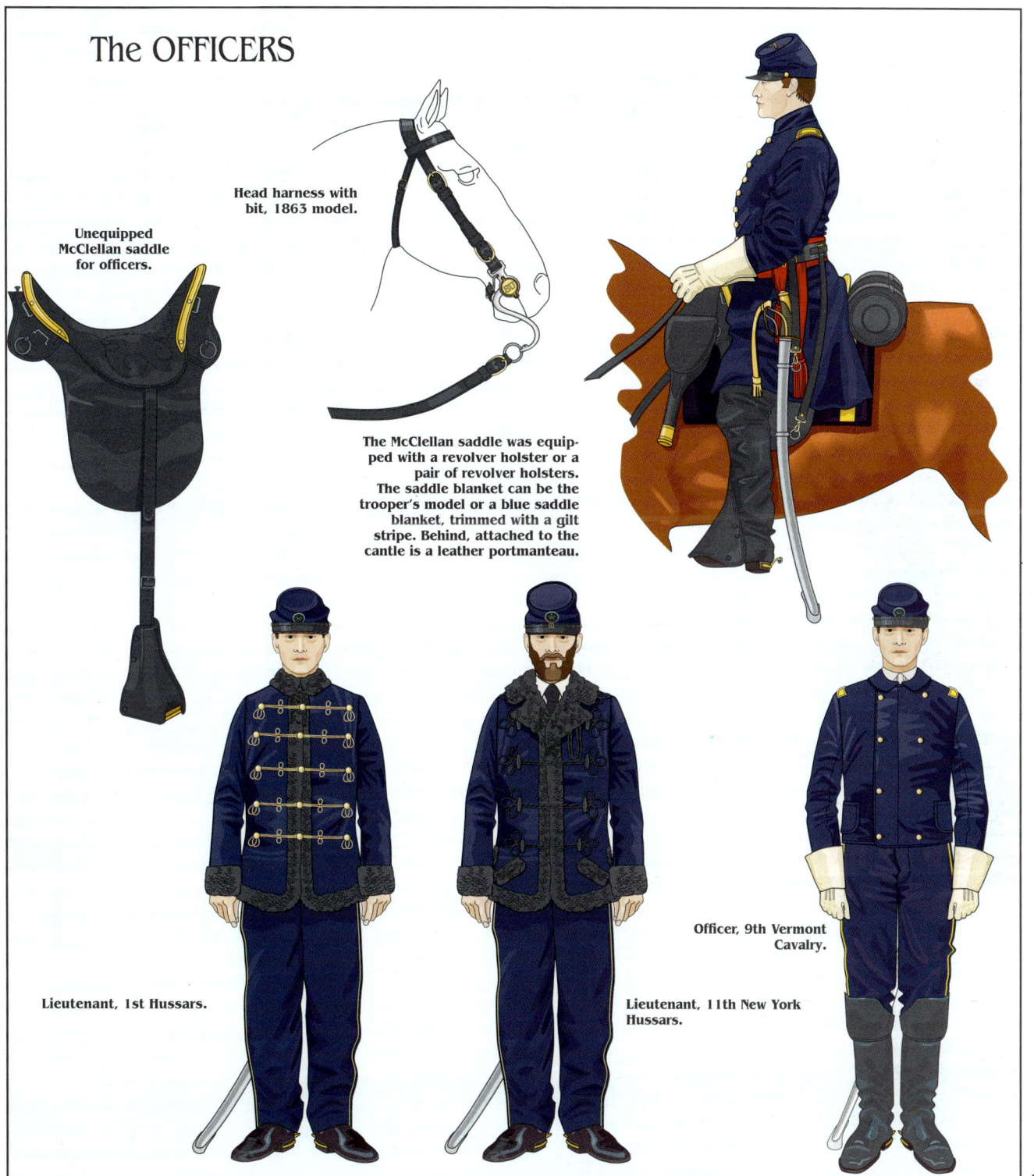

Unequipped McClellan saddle for officers.

Head harness with bit, 1863 model.

The McClellan saddle was equipped with a revolver holster or a pair of revolver holsters. The saddle blanket can be the trooper's model or a blue saddle blanket, trimmed with a gilt stripe. Behind, attached to the cantle is a leather portmanteau.

Lieutenant, 1st Hussars.

Lieutenant, 11th New York Hussars.

Officer, 9th Vermont Cavalry.

17

The EMBLEMS

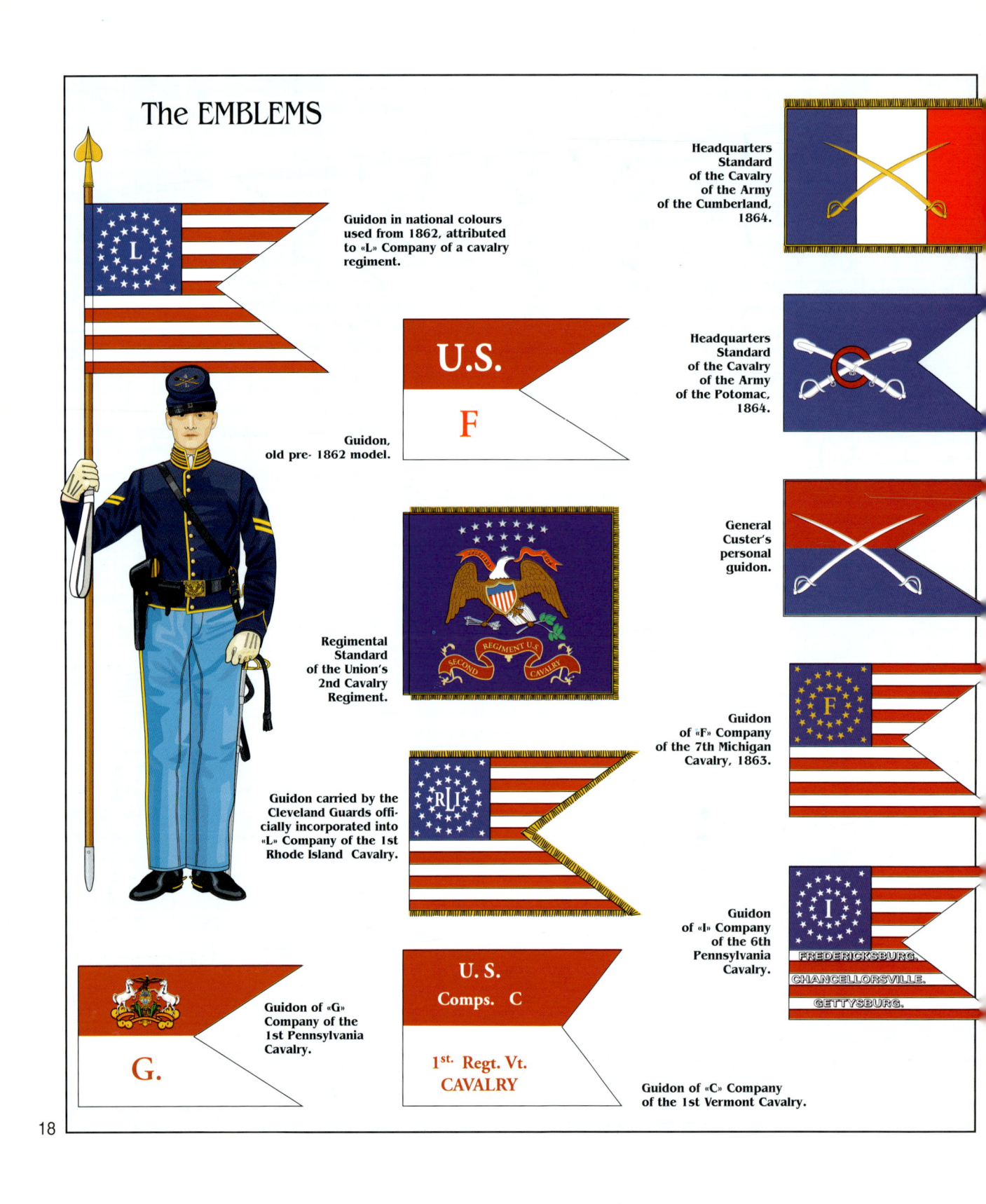

Guidon in national colours used from 1862, attributed to «L» Company of a cavalry regiment.

Headquarters Standard of the Cavalry of the Army of the Cumberland, 1864.

Guidon, old pre-1862 model.

Headquarters Standard of the Cavalry of the Army of the Potomac, 1864.

Regimental Standard of the Union's 2nd Cavalry Regiment.

General Custer's personal guidon.

Guidon carried by the Cleveland Guards officially incorporated into «L» Company of the 1st Rhode Island Cavalry.

Guidon of «F» Company of the 7th Michigan Cavalry, 1863.

Guidon of «I» Company of the 6th Pennsylvania Cavalry.

Guidon of «G» Company of the 1st Pennsylvania Cavalry.

Guidon of «C» Company of the 1st Vermont Cavalry.

THE UNION ARTILLERY

The artillery was organised into Heavy Artillery and Field Artillery, itself divided into Light Artillery and Horse Artillery.

The tendency during the Civil War was to concentrate close support at infantry or cavalry division level, with several batteries concentrated within an artillery brigade, under the command of a senior officer. To this was added a second artillery corps, the «Reserve», under the command of a General officer.

At the beginning of the conflict, the Union had 5 artillery regiments and 19 independant batteries. During the war, 52 regiments, 22 companies, and 1 647 batteries — all volunteers — were created and reorganised into 78 artillery regiments and 2 artillery companies.

In order to respond to the artillery's need for mobility, a good number of heavy artillery regiments were transformed into field artillery units and certain infantry regiments were changed into artillery regiments

The equipment used was divided into four categories:

— Field cannon.

— Howitzers which were mounted on interchangeable carriages and wheel units for at least seven types of cannon.

— Mortars, of which some of the bigger calibres were mounted directly on railway waggons.

— Fortress and coastal defence pieces.

Garrison artillerymen dressed like the infantry and were distinguished by the red piping on their trousers and the braided cord on their hats. They also wore a specific insignia on their headgear.

The field artillery was dressed like the cavalry. It remained however in full dress, with its dark blue shako and weeping willow plume.

THE ARTILLERY REGIMENT

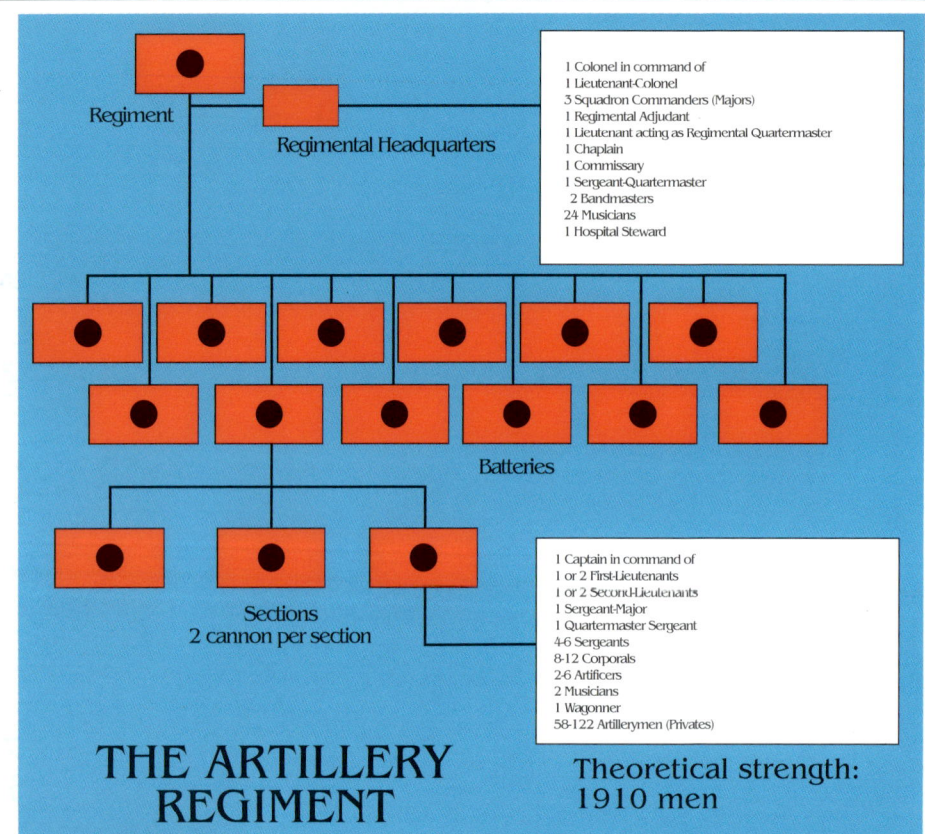

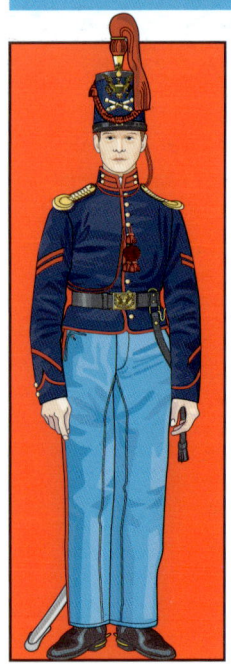

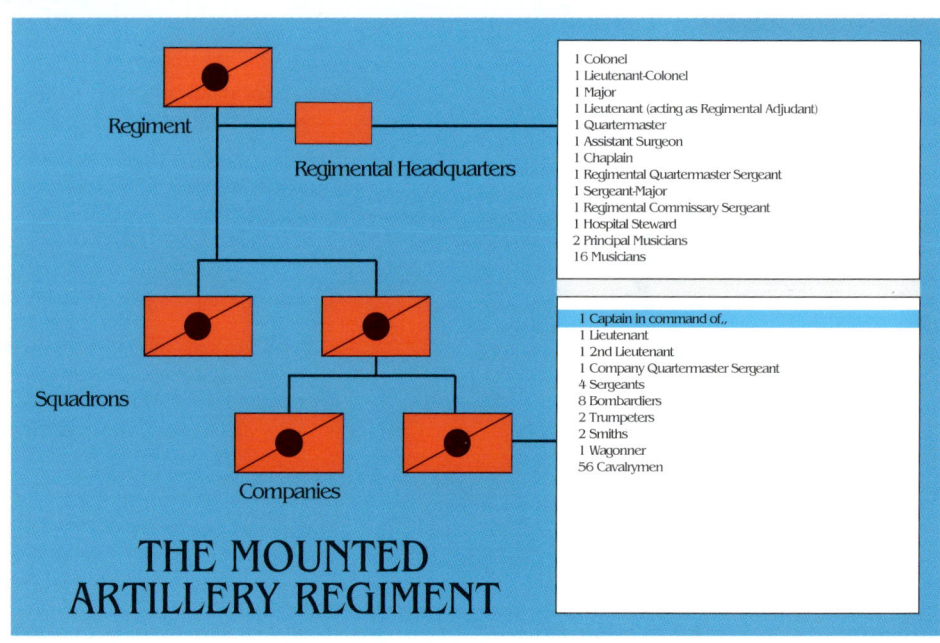

Regimental Headquarters:
- 1 Colonel in command of
- 1 Lieutenant-Colonel
- 3 Squadron Commanders (Majors)
- 1 Regimental Adjutant
- 1 Lieutenant acting as Regimental Quartermaster
- 1 Chaplain
- 1 Commissary
- 1 Sergeant-Quartermaster
- 2 Bandmasters
- 24 Musicians
- 1 Hospital Steward

Batteries

Sections — 2 cannon per section
- 1 Captain in command of
- 1 or 2 First-Lieutenants
- 1 or 2 Second-Lieutenants
- 1 Sergeant-Major
- 1 Quartermaster Sergeant
- 4-6 Sergeants
- 8-12 Corporals
- 2-6 Artificers
- 2 Musicians
- 1 Wagonner
- 58-122 Artillerymen (Privates)

Theoretical strength: 1910 men

THE MOUNTED ARTILLERY REGIMENT

Regimental Headquarters:
- 1 Colonel
- 1 Lieutenant-Colonel
- 1 Major
- 1 Lieutenant (acting as Regimental Adjutant)
- 1 Quartermaster
- 1 Assistant Surgeon
- 1 Chaplain
- 1 Regimental Quartermaster Sergeant
- 1 Sergeant-Major
- 1 Regimental Commissary Sergeant
- 1 Hospital Steward
- 2 Principal Musicians
- 16 Musicians

Squadrons

Companies
- 1 Captain in command of,,
- 1 Lieutenant
- 1 2nd Lieutenant
- 1 Company Quartermaster Sergeant
- 4 Sergeants
- 8 Bombardiers
- 2 Trumpeters
- 2 Smiths
- 1 Wagonner
- 56 Cavalrymen

FULL DRESS

Corporal.

Non-Commissioned Officer.

Drummer.

Bandmaster, although belonging to the artillery, this man is wearing a shako of the horse artillery.

Artilleryman in full dress, an 1858 regiment.

Musician.

NON-COMMISSIONED OFFICERS and OTHER RANKS

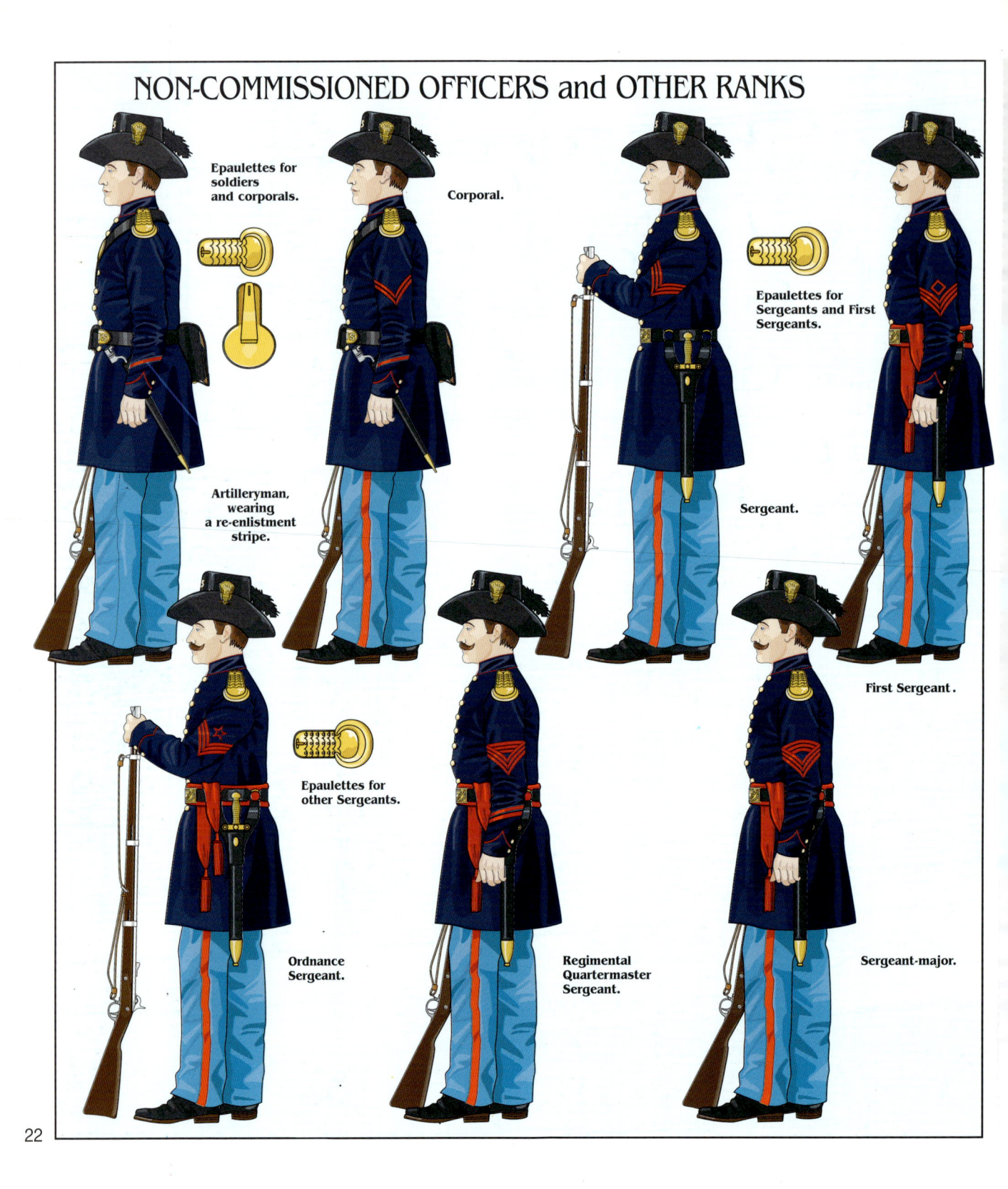

Epaulettes for soldiers and corporals.

Corporal.

Epaulettes for Sergeants and First Sergeants.

Artilleryman, wearing a re-enlistment stripe.

Sergeant.

First Sergeant.

Epaulettes for other Sergeants.

Ordnance Sergeant.

Regimental Quartermaster Sergeant.

Sergeant-major.

CLOTHING

Introduced by Captain W. Hardee, the parade hat was adopted by the whole army in 1858. The number indicated the regiment and the letter the battery.

Uniform Button.

Bummer.

Cap.

Forage Cap.

Shirt.

Jacket.

Full Dress Frock Coat. Particularly unwieldly, it was very quickly replaced by the Sack Coat or the Shell Jacket.

Braces.

Waistcoat.

Field Dress Sack Coat adopted by the Army of the United States in 1857.

Regulation Trousers with Non-Commissioned Officers' stripes.

EQUIPMENT

Bayonet belt and bayonet holder, cap pouch for soldiers and corporals.

Belt and its plate, non-commissioned officers' broadsword.

Metal flask covered with blue cloth. It could be brown or grey and marked «US». The bandolier was white cotton.

Cap pouch.

Natural wood or blue-painted flask, sometimes marked with the company's and its owner's regimental number. Leather strap or in stitched white cloth. There was also a quarter-litre metal beaker which was used for coffee and soup.

1855-model cartridge pouch with a metal box containing 58 cartridges. Sometimes the pouch could be worn on the belt.

Haversack, Keecham model, tarred cloth. It contains a sack inside for food..

Artilleryman's pouch containing fuses.

Artilleryman's bag containing tools and instruments for setting the cannon.

The Knackpsack, regulation model in leather and tarred cloth, was made up of two compartments folding down on each other, holding all the soldier's personal effects. The straps were made of black leather, or sometimes of natural leather.

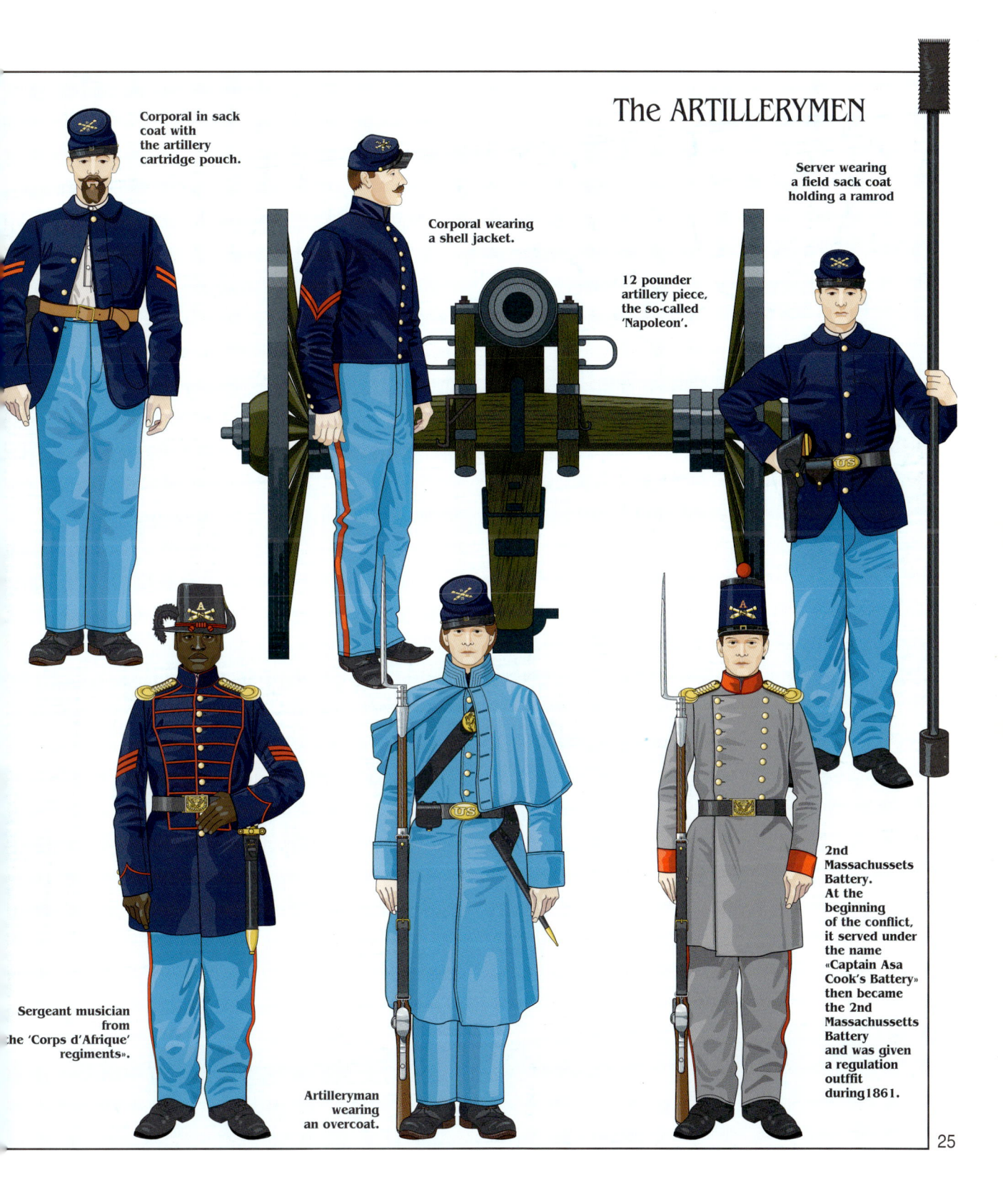

The ARTILLERYMEN

Corporal in sack coat with the artillery cartridge pouch.

Corporal wearing a shell jacket.

12 pounder artillery piece, the so-called 'Napoleon'.

Server wearing a field sack coat holding a ramrod

Sergeant musician from the 'Corps d'Afrique' regiments».

Artilleryman wearing an overcoat.

2nd Massachussets Battery. At the beginning of the conflict, it served under the name «Captain Asa Cook's Battery» then became the 2nd Massachussetts Battery and was given a regulation outffit during 1861.

The OFFICERS

Lieutenant in full dress wearing the light blue trousers adopted from 1861.

Lieutenant in service dress.

Lieutenant in service dress, rear view, wearing the regulation Frock Coat.

Lieutenant in Field dress.

Second-Lieutenant in frock coat and trousers, 1858 model. This was abandonned in 1861, but was often worn at the beginning of the conflict.

Second-Lieutenant in frock coat. Note the belt and the baldric stitched in white.

Lieutenant wearing a frock coat. Note the re-enlistment stripes which were only worn normally by the troopers and non-commissioned officers. Was this an officer risen from the ranks, allowed to wear these stripes?

26

OFFICERS' EQUIPMENT

A pair of binoculars and their case.

Belt and plate, revolver holster and cap pouch.

Hardee hat bearing the gold and black cord and tassel.

Haversack specially for officers.

Campaign dress bummer.

Lieutenant's full dress epaulette. The rank and the regiment are shown on the body, within a red circle.

Lieutenant wearing an overcoat with the removable cape.

1840 model artillery sabre.

Waistcoat.

Shoulder flaps showing rank.

Regulation trousers, dark blue until 1861, thereafter light blue.

Colonel

Lieutenant-Colonel

Major

Captain

Lieutenant

Second-Lieutenant

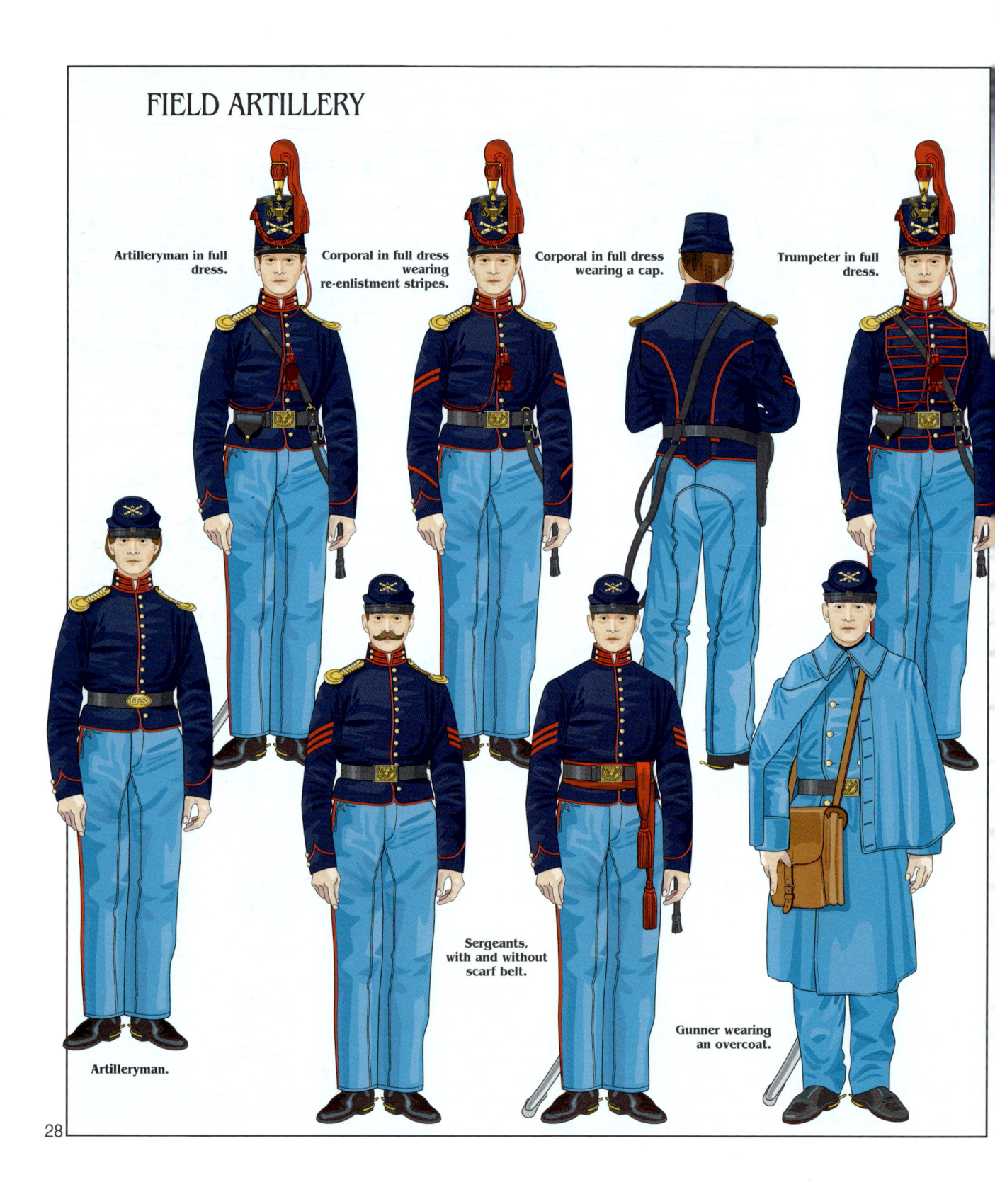

FIELD ARTILLERY

Artilleryman in full dress.

Corporal in full dress wearing re-enlistment stripes.

Corporal in full dress wearing a cap.

Trumpeter in full dress.

Artilleryman.

Sergeants, with and without scarf belt.

Gunner wearing an overcoat.

DRESS and EQUIPMENT

Trooper's and Non-Commissioned Officer's Shako.

Other models bear the national emblem with crossed cannon and the number of the regiment.

Bugle.

Bummer and cap.

Trumpeter's jacket.

Uniform button.

Epaulette with brass scales, for the troopers.

Artilleryman's regulation jacket.

Artilleryman's Regulation Shell Jacket. Like their comrades in the Foot Artillery, they wore the campaign jacket and sack coat.

Certain jacket were re-tailored by their owners, often the collar was lowered and a flap made to hold up the belt.

- Corporal
- Sergeant
- First Sergeant
- Ordnance Sergeant
- Quatermaster Sergeant
- Sergeant-Major

The stripes of rank are identical to those of the foot artillery.

Belt, baldric, plate, revolver holster, model 1840 artillery sabre.

Colt Navy revolver.

Regulation trousers for mounted troops with leather patches.

The LIGHT ARTILLERY OFFICERS

Junior officer in service dress.

Major in service dress.

Lieutenant in full dress.

The senior officers, major upwards, wore a tunic with a double row of buttons.

The officers of the Light Artillery had equipment and uniforms similar to the Heavy Artillery. They were distinguishable by their full dress shako, the Ringold cap which was kept on at their request when the Hardee Hat was introduced in 1858. As they were a mounted unit, the officers wore cavalry boots.

From 1860, the government allowed officers to wear a jacket with a special cut, which had Russian-style clover-shaped epaulettes which replaced the former marks of rank.

30

EMBLEMS

5th Artillery Regiment «C».
This flag was presented by the black citizens of Natchez (Mississippi) to the 9th Louisiana Volunteer Regiment, which became the 1st Artillery Regiment. The letter «C» meant coloured.

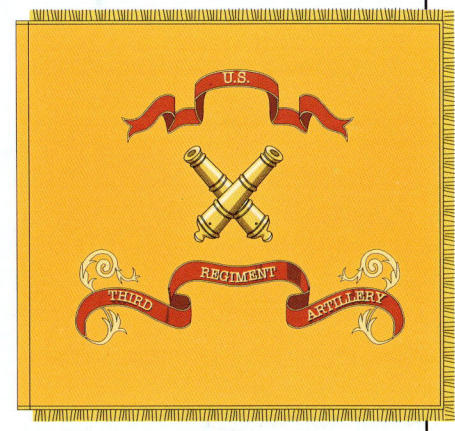

Regimental Flag of the 3rd Artillery Regiment.

Corporal Guidon-bearer, from a battery of «A» company of the 3rd Regiment of Field Artillery.

4th Battery, Massachusetts Field Artillery. This type of guidon with the national colours was given to the battery after the Battle of Bâton Rouge in Louisiana, for helping the 9th Connecticut Infantry capture several caissons of ammunition from the Southerners.

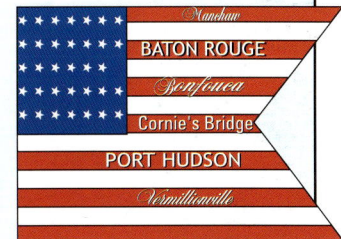

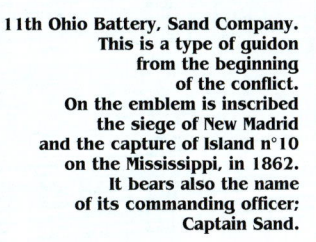

11th Ohio Battery, Sand Company. This is a type of guidon from the beginning of the conflict. On the emblem is inscribed the siege of New Madrid and the capture of Island n°10 on the Mississippi, in 1862. It bears also the name of its commanding officer: Captain Sand.

Regimental Flag (1864), of the 5th Pennsylvania Artillery Regiment which was officially the 204th Pennsylvania Volunteer Regiment.

1st Maine Artillery Regiment. 18th Maine Infantry Regiment became the 1st Artillery Regiment of the same state. After having been trained on artillery pieces in Washington DC, it was sent to Fort Sumter during the winter of 1863. A number of artillery regiments used this type of guidon to mark their positions.

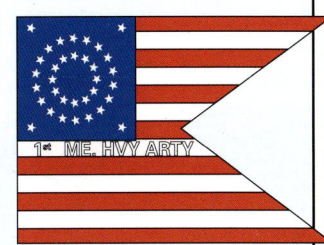

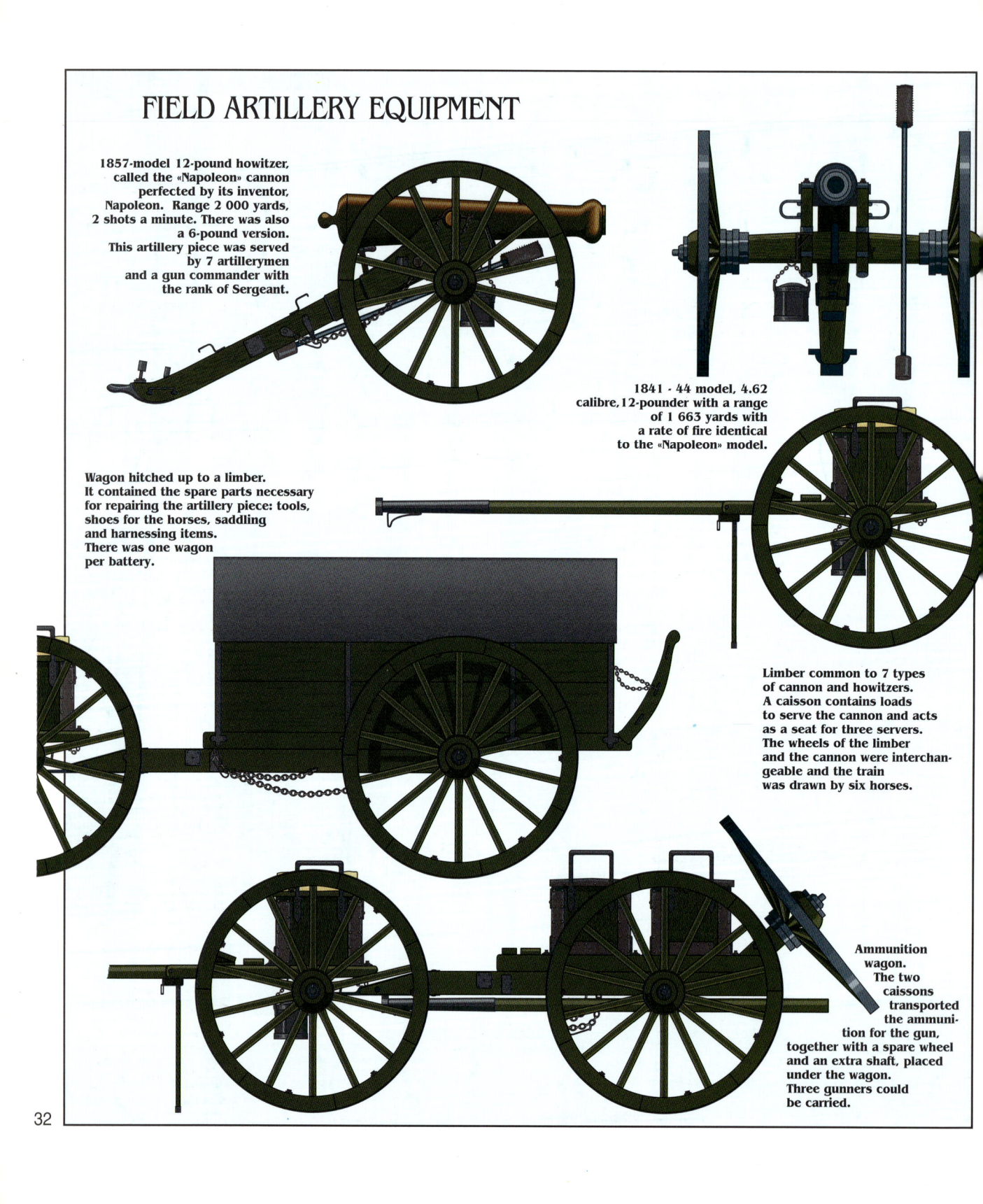

FIELD ARTILLERY EQUIPMENT

1857-model 12-pound howitzer, called the «Napoleon» cannon perfected by its inventor, Napoleon. Range 2 000 yards, 2 shots a minute. There was also a 6-pound version. This artillery piece was served by 7 artillerymen and a gun commander with the rank of Sergeant.

1841 - 44 model, 4.62 calibre, 12-pounder with a range of 1 663 yards with a rate of fire identical to the «Napoleon» model.

Wagon hitched up to a limber. It contained the spare parts necessary for repairing the artillery piece: tools, shoes for the horses, saddling and harnessing items. There was one wagon per battery.

Limber common to 7 types of cannon and howitzers. A caisson contains loads to serve the cannon and acts as a seat for three servers. The wheels of the limber and the cannon were interchangeable and the train was drawn by six horses.

Ammunition wagon. The two caissons transported the ammunition for the gun, together with a spare wheel and an extra shaft, placed under the wagon. Three gunners could be carried.

32

SOME ARTILLERY TACTICS

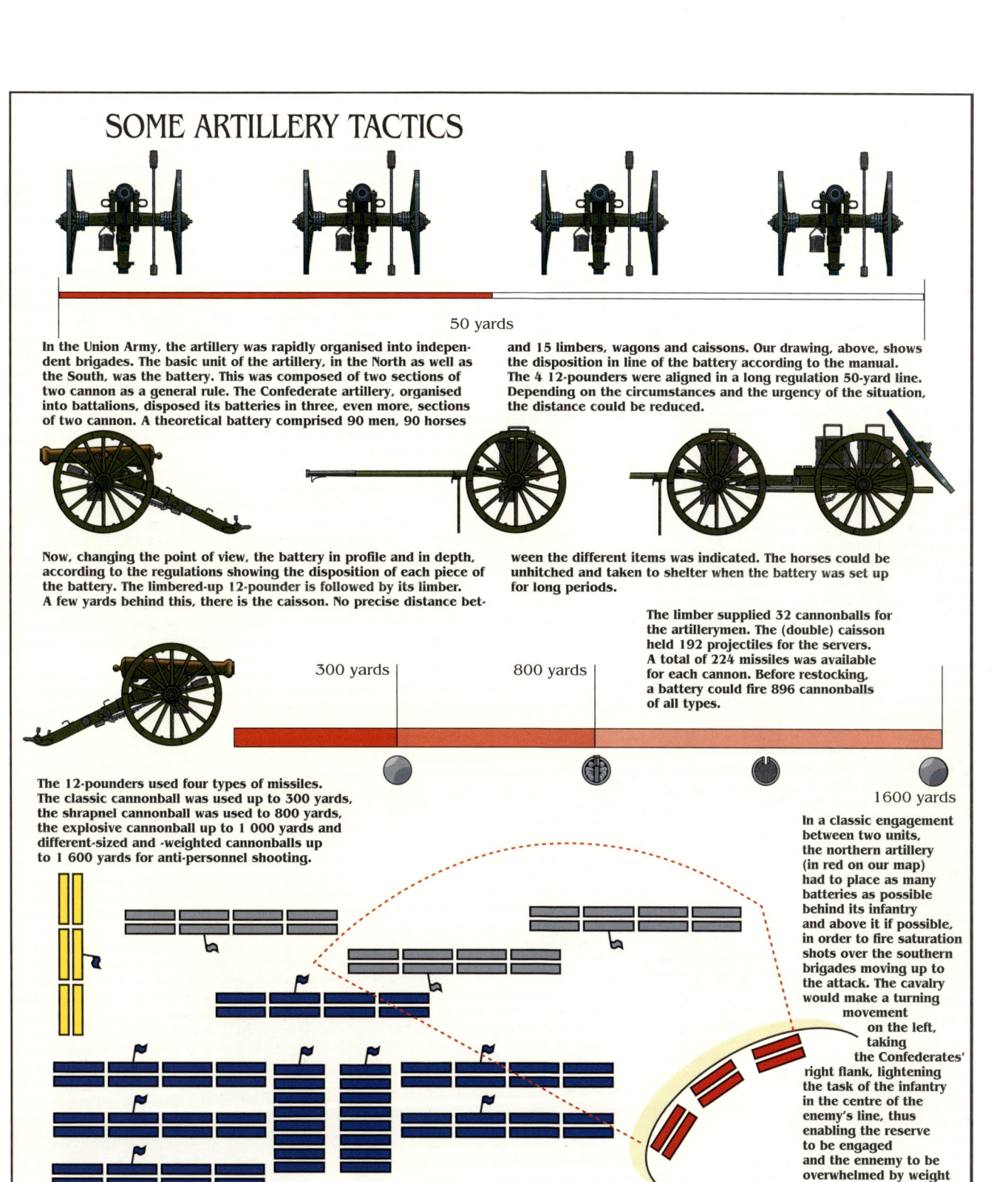

50 yards

In the Union Army, the artillery was rapidly organised into independent brigades. The basic unit of the artillery, in the North as well as the South, was the battery. This was composed of two sections of two cannon as a general rule. The Confederate artillery, organised into battalions, disposed its batteries in three, even more, sections of two cannon. A theoretical battery comprised 90 men, 90 horses and 15 limbers, wagons and caissons. Our drawing, above, shows the disposition in line of the battery according to the manual. The 4 12-pounders were aligned in a long regulation 50-yard line. Depending on the circumstances and the urgency of the situation, the distance could be reduced.

Now, changing the point of view, the battery in profile and in depth, according to the regulations showing the disposition of each piece of the battery. The limbered-up 12-pounder is followed by its limber. A few yards behind this, there is the caisson. No precise distance between the different items was indicated. The horses could be unhitched and taken to shelter when the battery was set up for long periods.

The limber supplied 32 cannonballs for the artillerymen. The (double) caisson held 192 projectiles for the servers. A total of 224 missiles was available for each cannon. Before restocking, a battery could fire 896 cannonballs of all types.

300 yards 800 yards 1600 yards

The 12-pounders used four types of missiles. The classic cannonball was used up to 300 yards, the shrapnel cannonball was used to 800 yards, the explosive cannonball up to 1 000 yards and different-sized and -weighted cannonballs up to 1 600 yards for anti-personnel shooting.

In a classic engagement between two units, the northern artillery (in red on our map) had to place as many batteries as possible behind its infantry and above it if possible, in order to fire saturation shots over the southern brigades moving up to the attack. The cavalry would make a turning movement on the left, taking the Confederates' right flank, lightening the task of the infantry in the centre of the enemy's line, thus enabling the reserve to be engaged and the ennemy to be overwhelmed by weight of numbers.

UNION ARMY SERVICES

THE ENGINEERS

APART FROM THE THREE FIGHTING ARMS, the infantry, the cavalry and the artillery, the United States Army had an Engineer Corps responsible for building bridges and fortifications and destroying those of the South.

The Engineer Corps was organised into 4 battalions comprising 7 senior officers with a Colonel in command, 42 junior officers, 40 Non-Commissioned Officers, 40 Corporals, 8 Musicians, 256 artificers, 256 soldiers.

From 1863, a Brigadier-General commanded the Corps, whose numbers were considerably increased. The Engineers served in the different armies of the Union and in the defence of Washington. Certain infantry regiments, notably from the Army of the Cumberland, were detached to serve with the Engineers, in addition to some volunteer units, like the 1st and 2nd New York Engineer Volunteers.

The Engineers were dressed and were ranked like the artillery, with a yellow distinctive. Their symbol was a castle with two towers.

The officers were considered as Staff officers with the two-towered castle distinctive embroidered in silver on the cap.

THE ORDNANCE SERVICE

This service looked after the maintenance, reparation and distribution of the weapons and ammunition.

The troopers and the non-commissioned officers were dressed like the artillery with crimson as the distinctive colour; the symbol was a burning grenade. The officers were dressed like Staff officers with the same distinctives and the button of the arm.

THE CARTOGRAPHER SERVICE

The Cartographer Service was entirely made up of officers responsible for reconnoitering, making and up-dating maps. The Corps was commanded by a Colonel and comprised 2 Lieutenant-Colonels, 8 Majors, 10 Captains and 13 Lieutenants. However, because their tasks were similar to those of the Engineers, the officers from this corps were often seconded to the other service and vice versa. With the spread of the conflict, civilians were also drafted in to help prepare maps. The Cartographer Service was attached directly to Headquarters.

UNION ARMY SERVICES

The officers wore the uniform of the Staff officers with their distinctive.

Military Railways

Trains were an important strategic element in the Civil War. From the first months of the conflict, the Confederates attacked the Northern railway lines intending to destroy the North's war industry. On the 31 January 1862, the US Congress created the USMRR (the US Military Rail Road) and authorised the President to nationalise the railway and the telegraph companies, and to take on their employees in the service of the state. Soldiers used on the railways were very quickly replaced by civilians, supervised by military engineers.

The USMRR was essentially a civilain organisation and wore neither uniform nor insignia. The soldiers affected to the trains wore their normal uniforms.

Military Telegraphs

In the first months of 1861, the State Department for War took control of the private telegraph services. Anton Strager was appointed Colonel in Chief responsible for the Telegraph Service, assisted by an «Assistant Quartermaster» and officers responsible for the lines. The telegraphers were responsible for the operation and the setting up of the lines. Except for the officers who wore staff uniforms. the telegraphers were civilians; however in order not to be taken for spies by the Confederates, it was decided from 1864 onwards to give them sky blue tunics and trousers, with a silver stripe and a cap with a silver chin-strap.

Signals

Before the war, Major A.J. Meyer had experimented with a system of messages transmitted by flags and torches. He was given the responsibility for transmitting and establishing the transmission of messages in the shortest time possible and in the worst possible weather.

A signals detachment commanded by a captain with 20 men were attached to each Army Corps Headquarters. They were also responsible for setting up and maintaining the telegraph lines.

The soldiers wore cavalry uniforms without the distinctive, but with an insignia embroidered on the left sleeve. Signals officers wore staff officers' uniforms from 1864, with an insignia for their function.

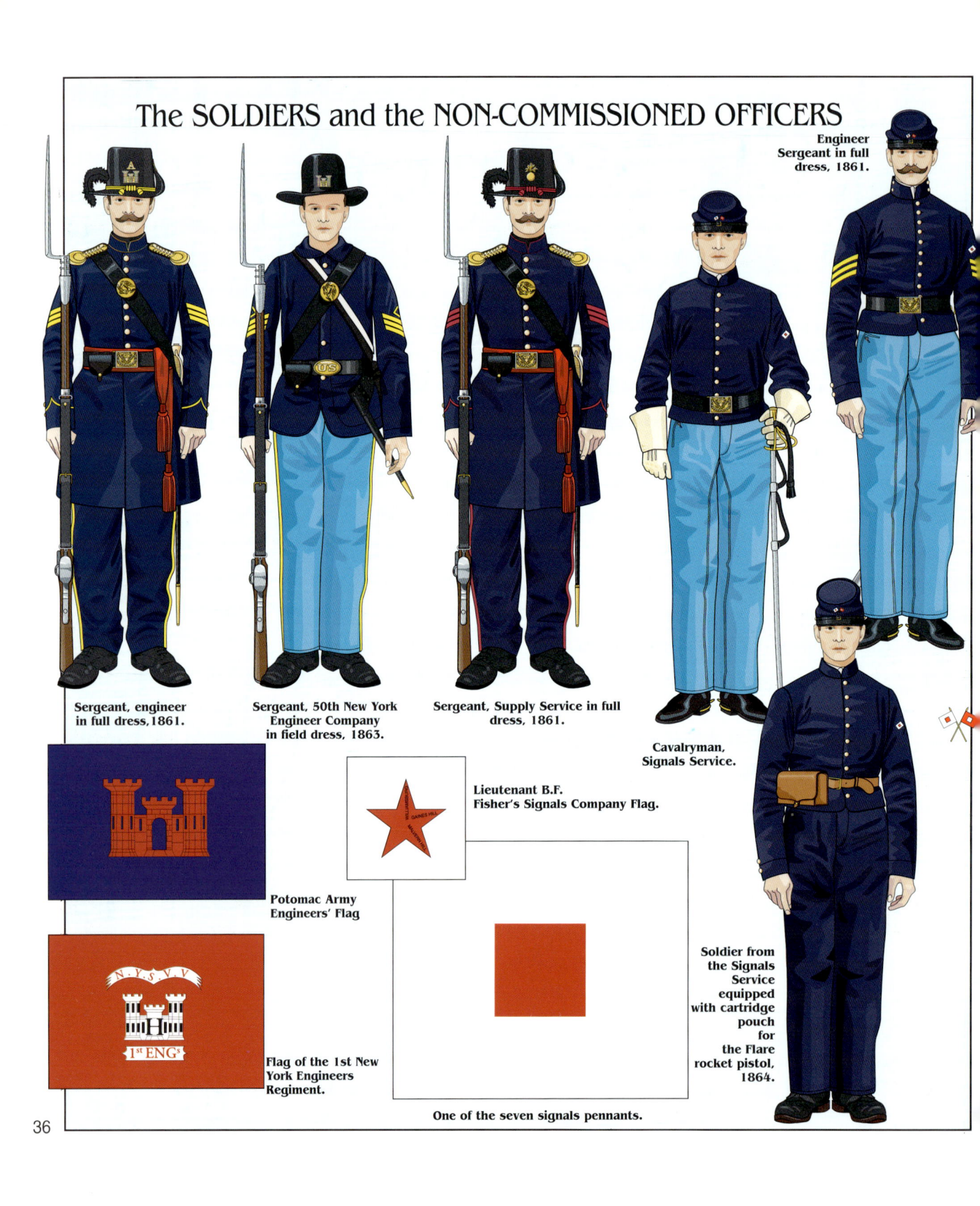

The SOLDIERS and the NON-COMMISSIONED OFFICERS

Sergeant, engineer in full dress, 1861.

Sergeant, 50th New York Engineer Company in field dress, 1863.

Sergeant, Supply Service in full dress, 1861.

Cavalryman, Signals Service.

Engineer Sergeant in full dress, 1861.

Potomac Army Engineers' Flag.

Lieutenant B.F. Fisher's Signals Company Flag.

Flag of the 1st New York Engineers Regiment.

One of the seven signals pennants.

Soldier from the Signals Service equipped with cartridge pouch for the Flare rocket pistol, 1864.

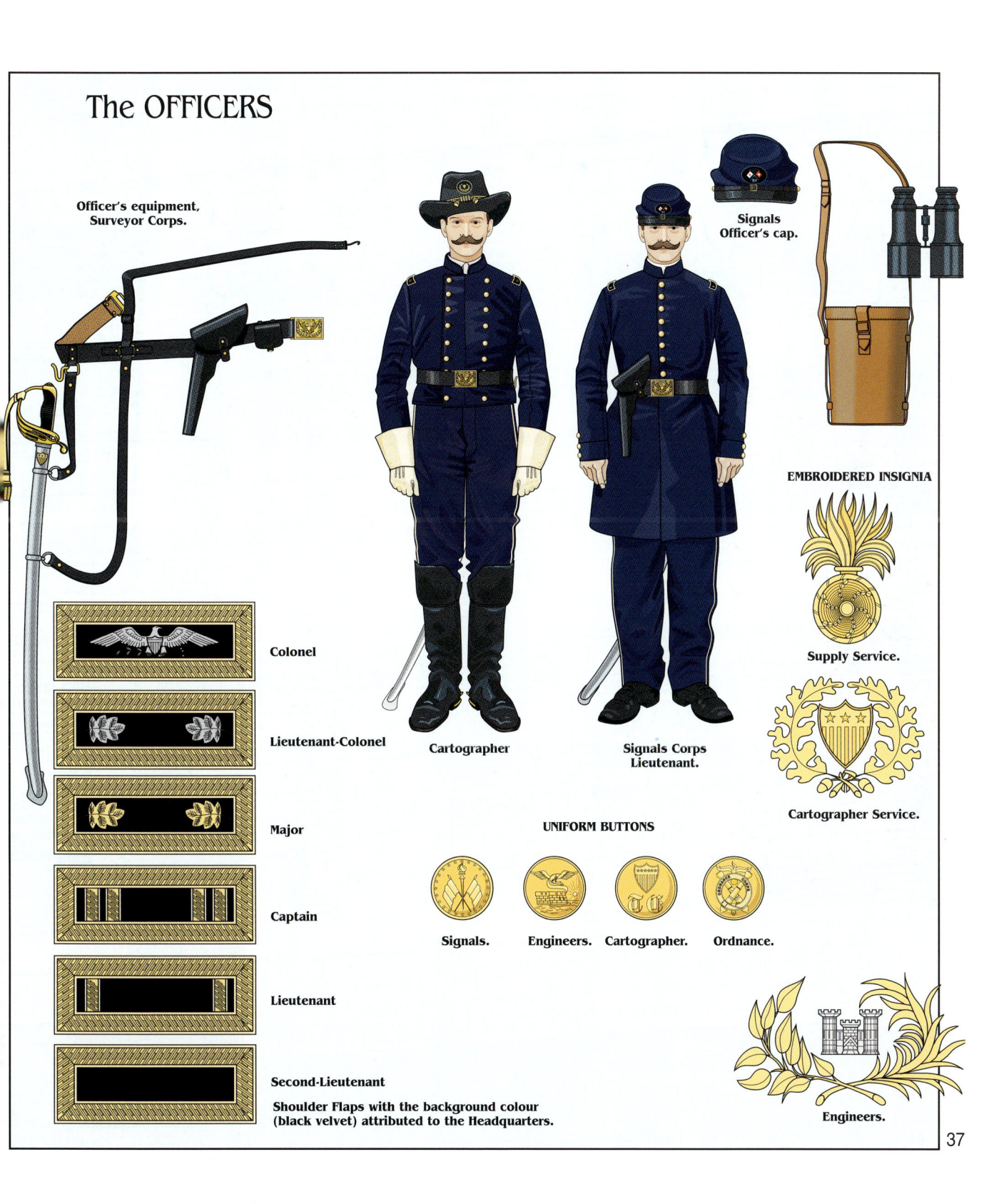

The OFFICERS

Officer's equipment, Surveyor Corps.

Colonel

Lieutenant-Colonel

Major

Captain

Lieutenant

Second-Lieutenant

Shoulder Flaps with the background colour (black velvet) attributed to the Headquarters.

Cartographer

Signals Corps Lieutenant.

Signals Officer's cap.

EMBROIDERED INSIGNIA

Supply Service.

Cartographer Service.

UNIFORM BUTTONS

Signals.   Engineers.   Cartographer.   Ordnance.

Engineers.

The MEDICAL SERVICE

In 1861, THE HEALTH SERVICE COMPRISED 30 surgeons with the rank of major and 84 assistants with the rank of Captain or Lieutenant. The department was responsible for the health services attached to the volunteer regiments.

From 1862, it was decentralised at Army Corps level and built its first hospital, finishing the conflict with 204 hospitals. An archive department was created to keep photographs and archives of casualties whose wounds needed special equipment, as well as photos of soldiers who had been invalided out, to prevent fraud.

Congress also authorised the hiring of doctors aged between 18 and 25 who had not finished their studies, ; after an examination, they were called "Medical Cadets" and obtained their second-lieutenant's commission later.

The Health Service includeded "Hospital Stewards" who had the rank of NCOs and who were responsible for managing field hospitals and looking after medicines.

To this was added an ambulanceman's Corps which in the Army of the Potomac, numbered 2 300 men and 60 officers.

The uniform of the surgeons was that of the staff officers with however a dark green scarf; rank shoulder flaps were black velvet with a green background with the embroidered initials "M.S.". The sword was the 1840-model which also equipped the Treasury Service.

Hospital Stewards were dressed according to regulations, with crimson as the distinctive colour and a green armband with a caduceus.

The MEDICAL CORPS

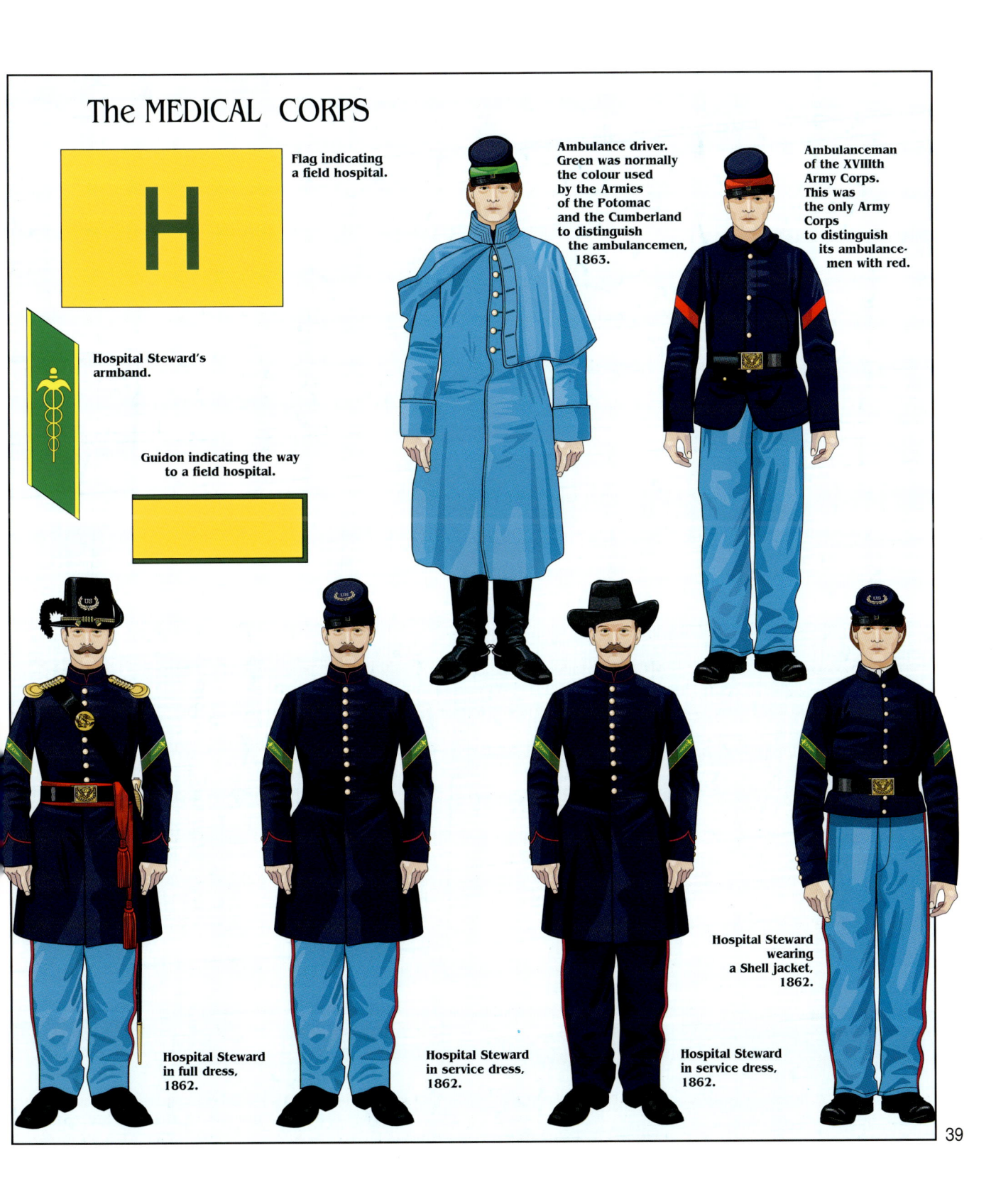

Flag indicating a field hospital.

Hospital Steward's armband.

Guidon indicating the way to a field hospital.

Ambulance driver. Green was normally the colour used by the Armies of the Potomac and the Cumberland to distinguish the ambulancemen, 1863.

Ambulanceman of the XVIIIth Army Corps. This was the only Army Corps to distinguish its ambulancemen with red.

Hospital Steward in full dress, 1862.

Hospital Steward in service dress, 1862.

Hospital Steward in service dress, 1862.

Hospital Steward in service dress, 1862.

Hospital Steward wearing a Shell jacket, 1862.

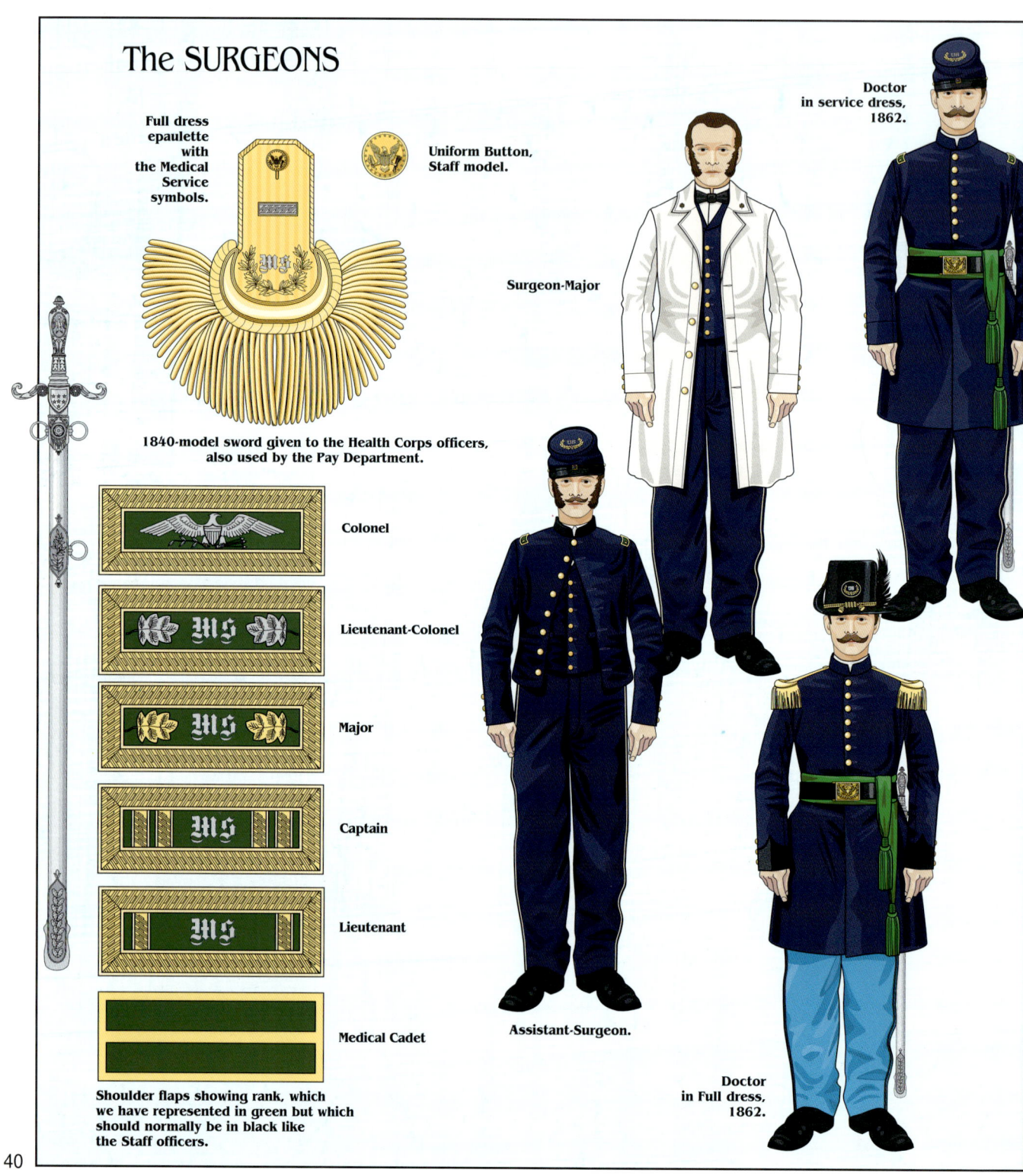

The SURGEONS

Full dress epaulette with the Medical Service symbols.

Uniform Button, Staff model.

1840-model sword given to the Health Corps officers, also used by the Pay Department.

Colonel

Lieutenant-Colonel

Major

Captain

Lieutenant

Medical Cadet

Shoulder flaps showing rank, which we have represented in green but which should normally be in black like the Staff officers.

Surgeon-Major

Doctor in service dress, 1862.

Assistant-Surgeon.

Doctor in Full dress, 1862.

GENERAL OFFICERS

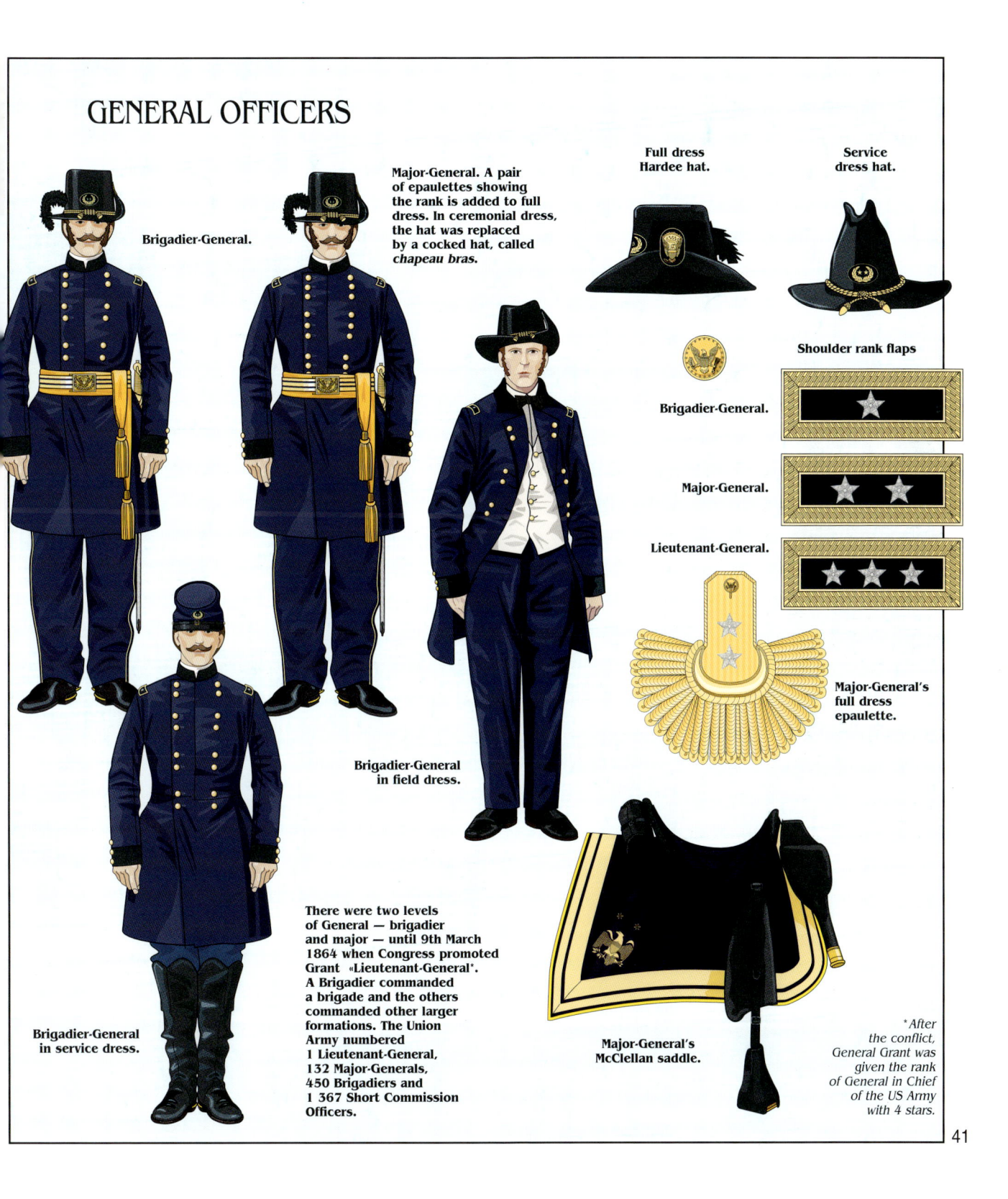

Brigadier-General.

Major-General. A pair of epaulettes showing the rank is added to full dress. In ceremonial dress, the hat was replaced by a cocked hat, called *chapeau bras*.

Full dress Hardee hat.

Service dress hat.

Brigadier-General.

Brigadier-General in field dress.

Shoulder rank flaps

Brigadier-General.

Major-General.

Lieutenant-General.

Major-General's full dress epaulette.

Brigadier-General in service dress.

There were two levels of General — brigadier and major — until 9th March 1864 when Congress promoted Grant «Lieutenant-General*. A Brigadier commanded a brigade and the others commanded other larger formations. The Union Army numbered 1 Lieutenant-General, 132 Major-Generals, 450 Brigadiers and 1 367 Short Commission Officers.

Major-General's McClellan saddle.

*After the conflict, General Grant was given the rank of General in Chief of the US Army with 4 stars.

41

The CONFEDERATE CAVALRY

Immediately after the Secession was declared and an army set up, all the South's volunteers wanted to enlist in the cavalry. Indeed, the population was mainly rural and well versed in the art of riding horses from an early age.

A cavalry regiment comprised 10 companies of 60-100 horsemen.

The organisation of a regiment was more or less like that of the Union. At first the cavalry was used as a rapid attack force but the High Command decided that the Army of North Virginia would organise the regiments into cavalry corps of 5 - 7 regiments to which were attached an artillery brigade and an equipment train.

The Confederate cavalry was divided into 4 main parts, the regular cavalry; the "Partisan Rangers", of which the most famous were Colonel Mosby's, renowned for their daringly spectacular attacks on the Union's rear; the scouts, recruited mainly from the Indian Territories in the West, whose principal job was reconnoitering the Northern positions. Couriers ensured the transmission of orders at Headquarters level.

There was a dress order dated 6th June 1861 which gave a grey tunic, yellow caps with a dark blue stripe and sky blue trousers as the official colours of the uniform. In reality, this order was not obeyed very much since the cavalrymen had to supply the uniform themselves; they preferred to wear more fashionable gear, hussar dress or mexican hats, deerskin jackets and tunics in the Texan regiments, for example.

All this gave the Confederate cavalry a rather disparate appearance which, as the blockade took effect, gave way progressively to the butternut and to clothes cut out of mattress cloth.

As the Confederate Cavalryman had to equip himself and come with his own horse, saddles, like the weapons, came from different sources. Apart from copies of Northern weapons, there were individual weapons, imported and captured.

THE CONFEDERATE CAVALRY

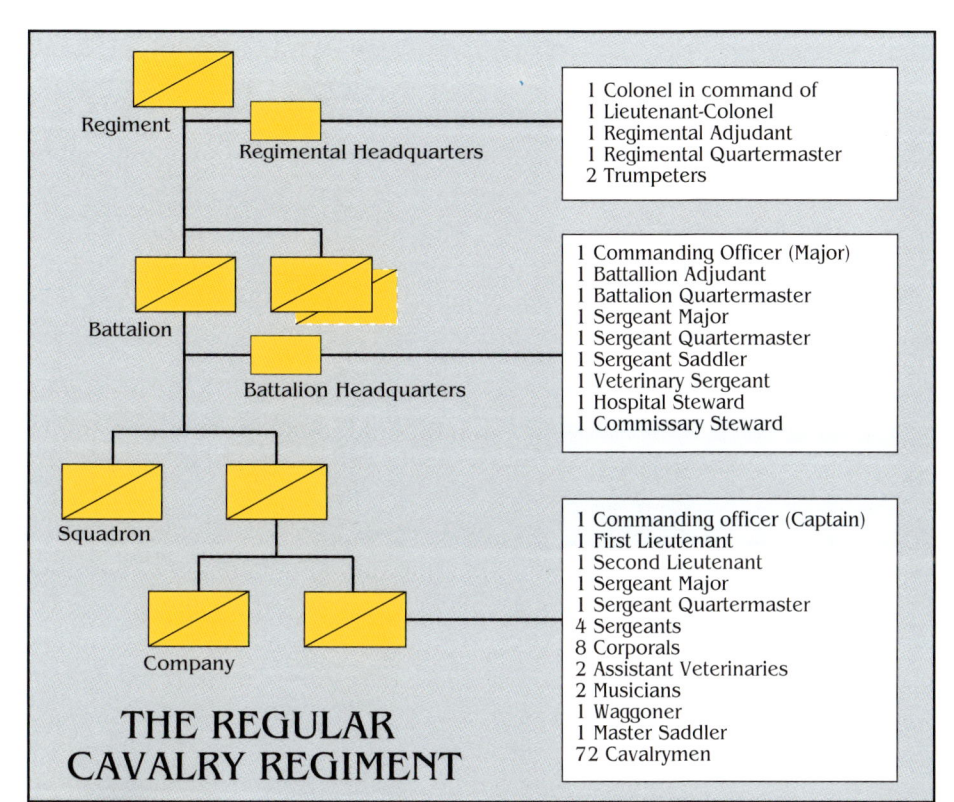

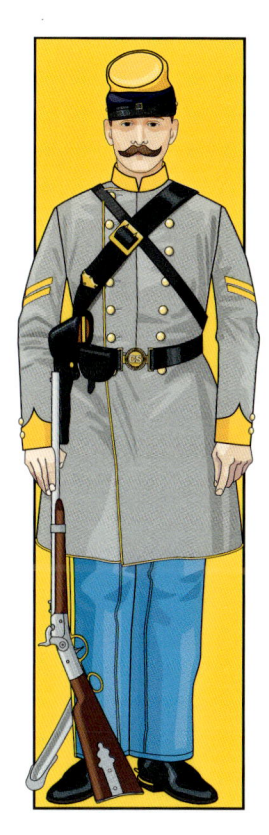

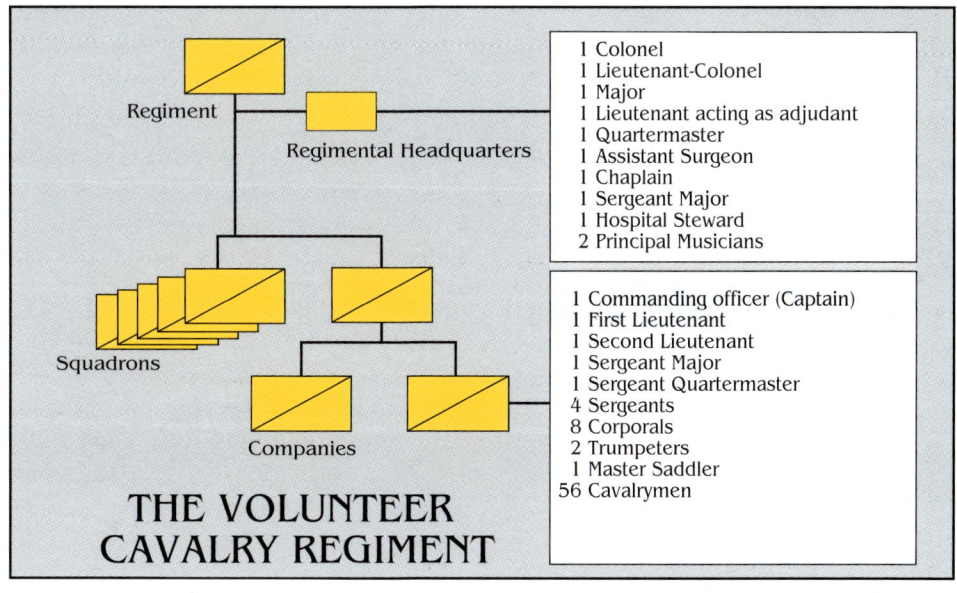

THE REGULAR CAVALRY REGIMENT

Regiment — Regimental Headquarters:
1 Colonel in command of
1 Lieutenant-Colonel
1 Regimental Adjudant
1 Regimental Quartermaster
2 Trumpeters

Battalion — Battalion Headquarters:
1 Commanding Officer (Major)
1 Battallion Adjudant
1 Battalion Quartermaster
1 Sergeant Major
1 Sergeant Quartermaster
1 Sergeant Saddler
1 Veterinary Sergeant
1 Hospital Steward
1 Commissary Steward

Squadron — Company:
1 Commanding officer (Captain)
1 First Lieutenant
1 Second Lieutenant
1 Sergeant Major
1 Sergeant Quartermaster
4 Sergeants
8 Corporals
2 Assistant Veterinaries
2 Musicians
1 Waggoner
1 Master Saddler
72 Cavalrymen

THE VOLUNTEER CAVALRY REGIMENT

Regiment — Regimental Headquarters:
1 Colonel
1 Lieutenant-Colonel
1 Major
1 Lieutenant acting as adjudant
1 Quartermaster
1 Assistant Surgeon
1 Chaplain
1 Sergeant Major
1 Hospital Steward
2 Principal Musicians

Squadrons — Companies:
1 Commanding officer (Captain)
1 First Lieutenant
1 Second Lieutenant
1 Sergeant Major
1 Sergeant Quartermaster
4 Sergeants
8 Corporals
2 Trumpeters
1 Master Saddler
56 Cavalrymen

The REGULAR CAVALRY

Cavalryman in regulation full dress.

Corporal in regulation full dress.

Corporal wearing an overcoat.

Sergeant wearing a shell jacket. The yellow stripes were often replaced by black ones.

Cavalryman wearing a shell jacket and pouches for the rifle and the revolver.

Corporal wearing a jacket. In the Confederate cavalry, the cap was often replaced by a hat. Leather equipment was plain as there was no polish of the right colour.

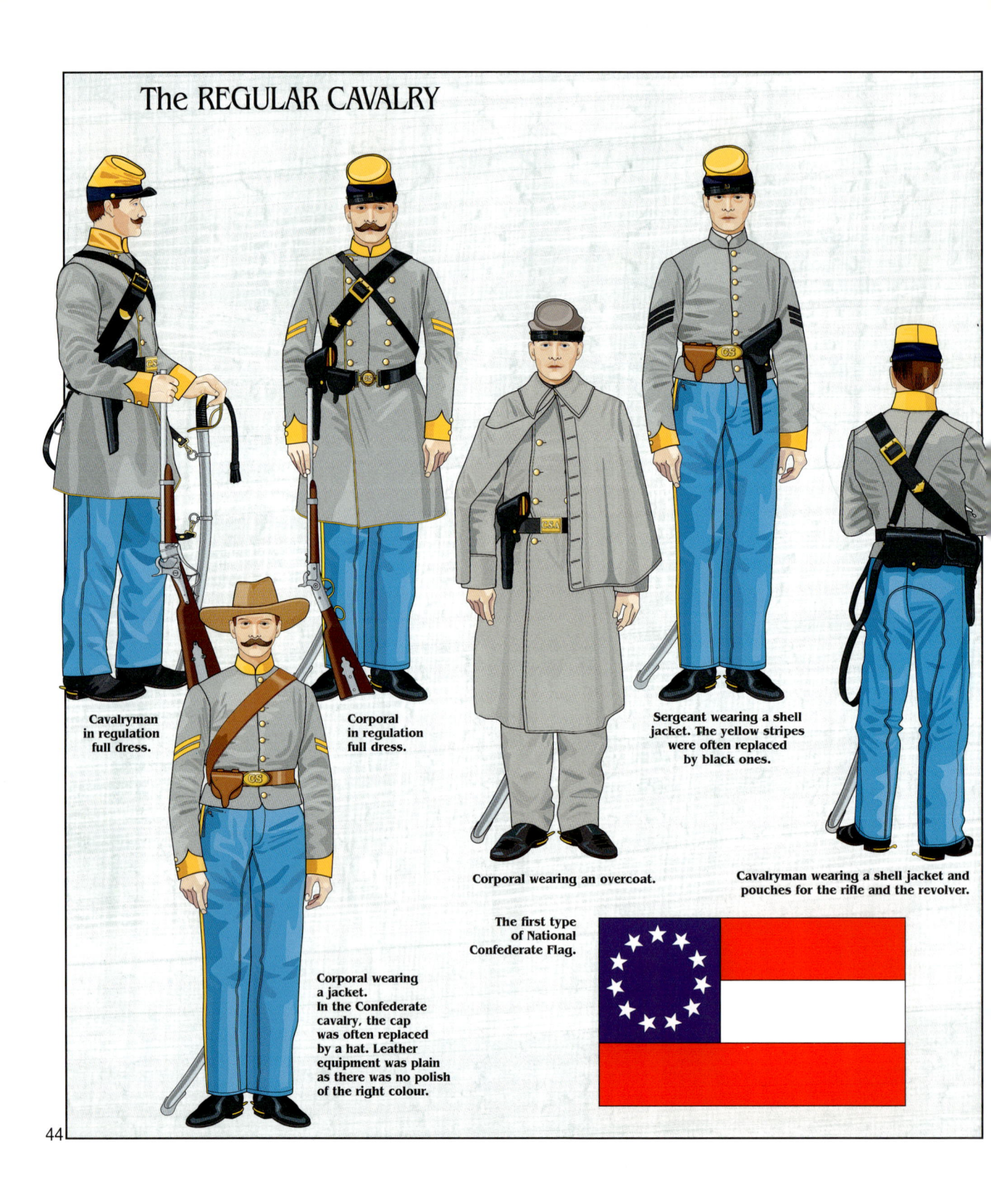

The first type of National Confederate Flag.

The RANKS in the CONFEDERATE CAVALRY

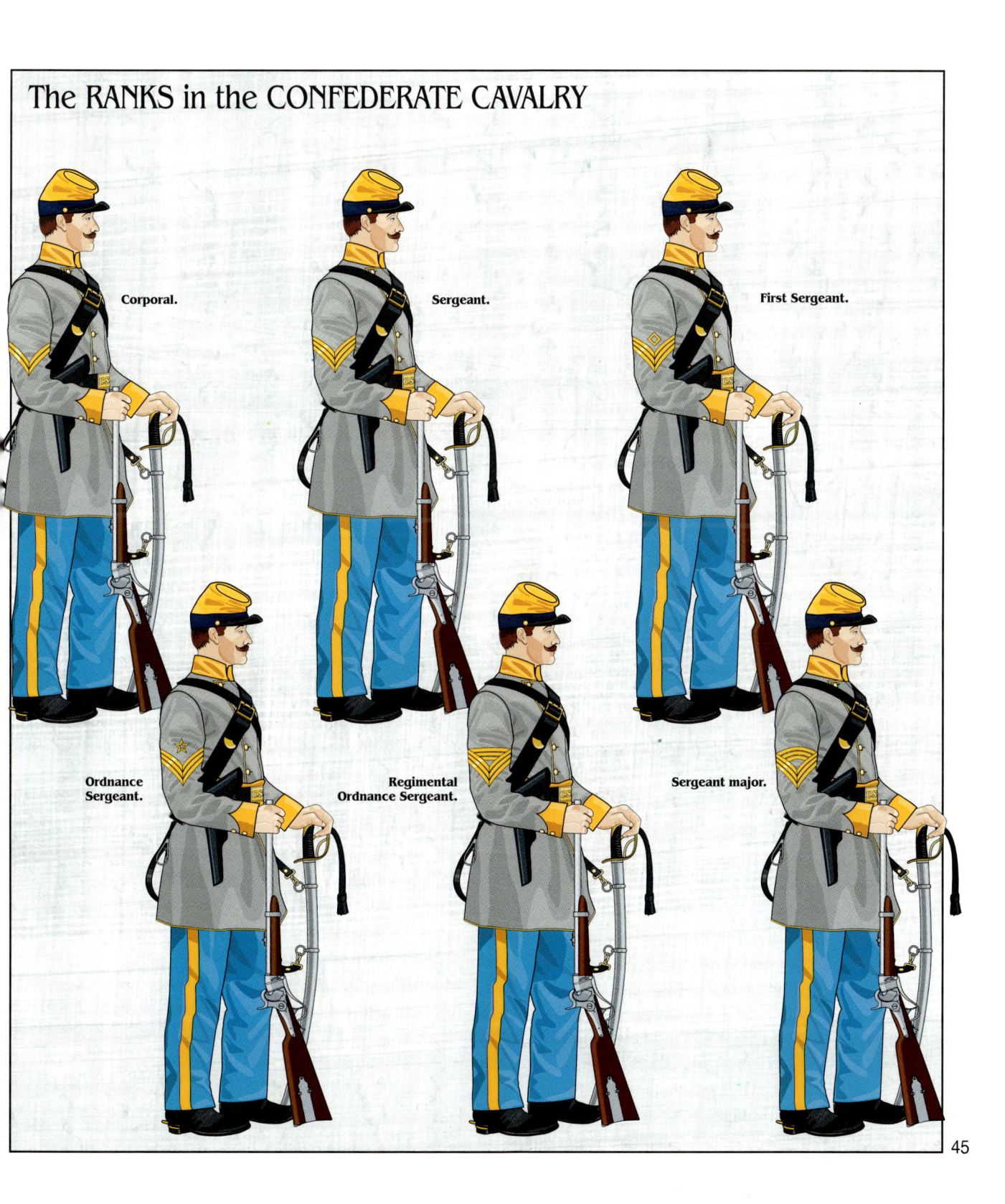

Corporal.

Sergeant.

First Sergeant.

Ordnance Sergeant.

Regimental Ordnance Sergeant.

Sergeant major.

45

EQUIPMENT

Regular Cavalryman's cap.

Regulation Jacket.

Wooden or metal flasks. There were mant different forms during the conflict, and the straps were cut out of the cloth of a haversack.

Cartridge pouches.

Regulation trousers worn from Corporal upwards. The ordinary cavalryman wore the same hide-lined trousers, but without the side stripe.

Boots.

Cavalry equipment. The South's armament industry basically copied the regulation weapons of the North's cavalry. However there was a great variety in the weapons used by the Confederates: those that were imported from England; personal weapons brought by the cavalrymen themselves (like the sawn-off shotgun, for example); and the regulation weapons. With the stiffening of the blockade, supplying black leather equipment became more and more difficult and the equipment was increasingly distributed in its natural colour, or even replaced by bandoliers and belts made from cloth.

The VOLUNTEER CAVALRYMEN

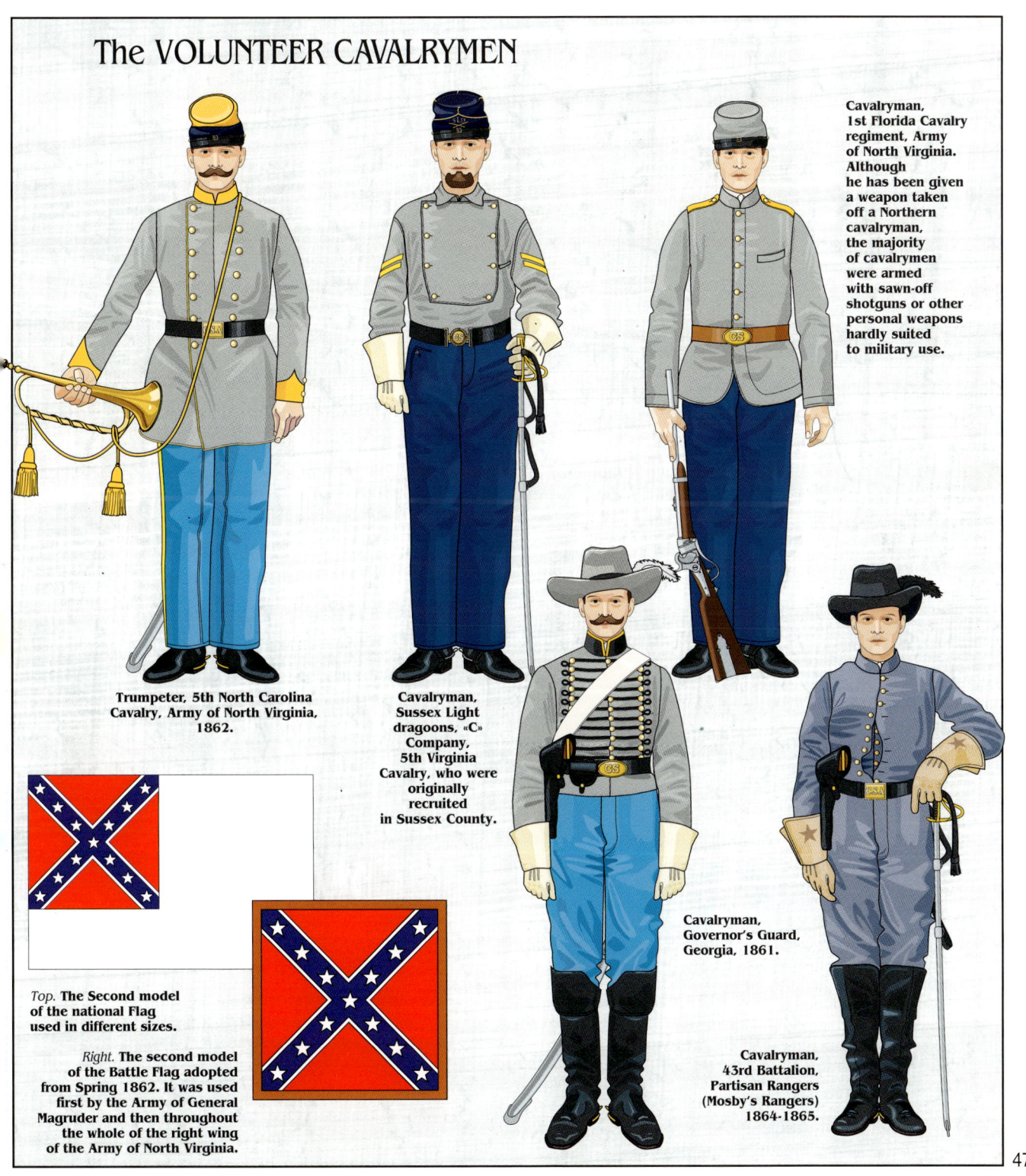

Cavalryman, 1st Florida Cavalry regiment, Army of North Virginia. Although he has been given a weapon taken off a Northern cavalryman, the majority of cavalrymen were armed with sawn-off shotguns or other personal weapons hardly suited to military use.

Trumpeter, 5th North Carolina Cavalry, Army of North Virginia, 1862.

Cavalryman, Sussex Light dragoons, «C» Company, 5th Virginia Cavalry, who were originally recruited in Sussex County.

Cavalryman, Governor's Guard, Georgia, 1861.

Cavalryman, 43rd Battalion, Partisan Rangers (Mosby's Rangers) 1864-1865.

Top. The Second model of the national Flag used in different sizes.

Right. The second model of the Battle Flag adopted from Spring 1862. It was used first by the Army of General Magruder and then throughout the whole of the right wing of the Army of North Virginia.

47

The VOLUNTEER CAVALRYMEN

Sergeant from General Beaufort's Troops, 1861.

Cavalryman from Hampton's Legion, 1861.

Guidon from a Texas cavalry regiment, 1861.

Sergeant, 1st Texas Cavalry (*Chasseurs à cheval du Texas*) 1861.

Battle Flag of General Parson's Texas Cavalry.

Cavalryman, 26th Texas Cavalry, or *Chasseurs à cheval* de Debray. Xavier Blanchard Debray was a Frenchman who had settled in the United States in 1852. Commissioned as Colonel, Debray was authorised to levy a cavalry regiment in which the French influence was heavily felt, particularly in details of dress, especially collar patches, green as a distinctive colour and the lance which was later replaced by a rifle.

The VOLUNTEER CAVALRYMEN

Cavalryman, 6th South Carolina Cavalry, 1863.

A group of three cavalrymen from the 8th Texas cavalry. The cavalryman in grey is wearing the regulation uniform. the corporal on his right is wearing field dress and the one in the middle is wearing dress often worn by cavalrymen. The jacket was replaced by a shirt. The Texas regiments were often characterised by their belt-plate bearing the Lone Star. After the war, they were to join the famous police force, the "Texas Rangers".

Cavalryman, 30th Texas Cavalry Regiment. This is a reconstruction from different articles of clothing.

Cavalryman from General Jeb Stuart's Brigade, reconstituted from black and white period photographs.

49

The VIRGINIA CAVALRY

Corporal, 1st Virginia Cavalry, better known under the name of the «Black Horse Cavalry», 1861.

Corporal, 1st Virginia Cavalry reconstituted from a black and white period photograph. On the document, the stripes and the frogs had to be passed over with chalk to give the illusion of yellow, which comes out black on period photographs.

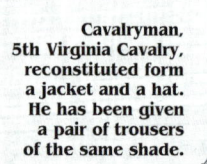

Cavalryman, 5th Virginia Cavalry, reconstituted form a jacket and a hat. He has been given a pair of trousers of the same shade.

Cavalryman, 6th Virginia Cavalry reconstituted from a black and white period photograph. The stripes on the shirt are doubtless yellow, the distinctive colour of the cavalry.

Cavalryman's tunic, 14th Virginia cavalry, about 1861.

Corporal, 12th Virginia Cavalry, 1864

Guidon, Smith's Dragoons, incorporated into the 5th Virginia cavalry.

FROM THE SMYTH LADIES.
GOD AND OUR RIGHT.

The OFFICER RANKS

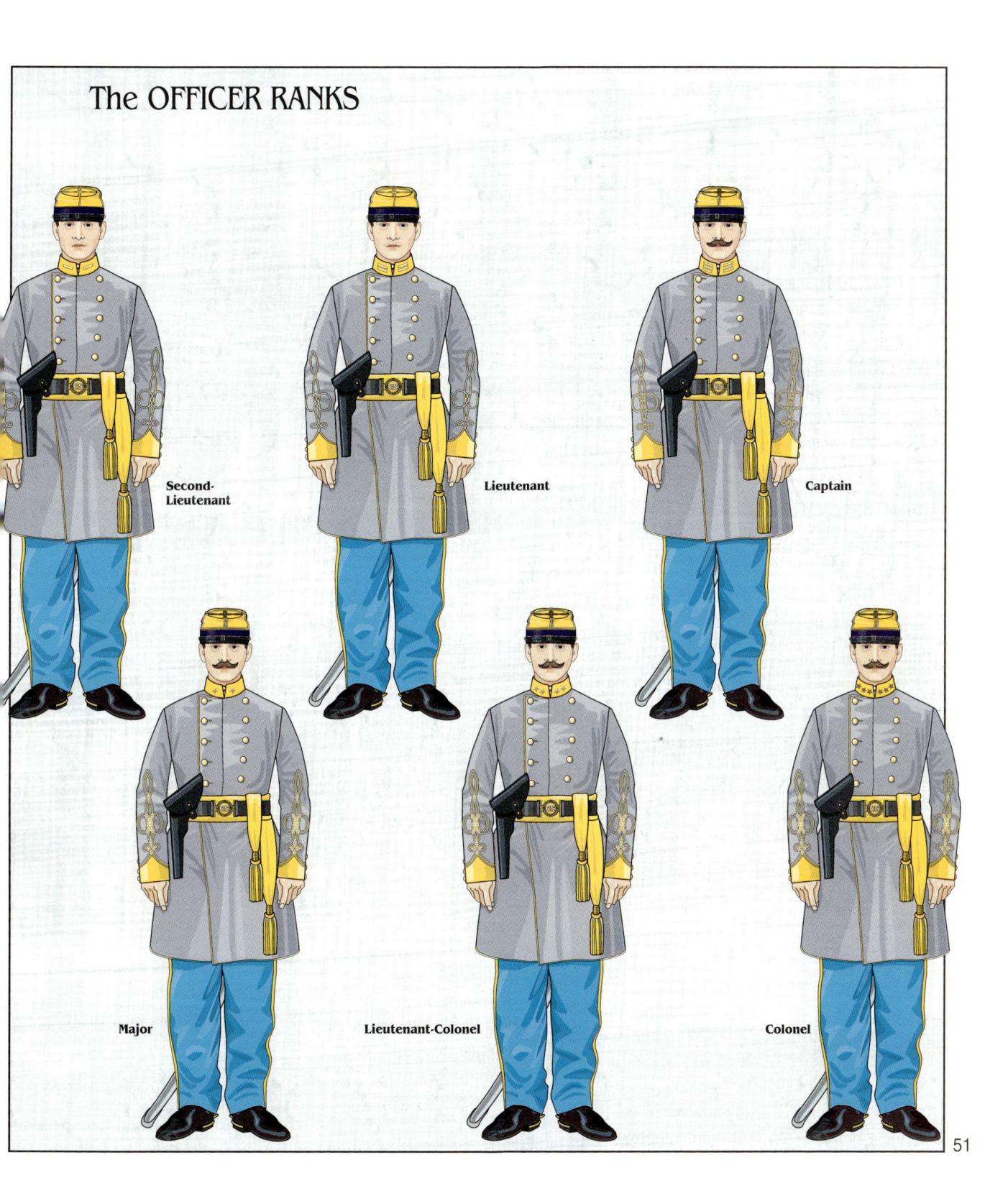

Second-Lieutenant

Lieutenant

Captain

Major

Lieutenant-Colonel

Colonel

THE OFFICERS

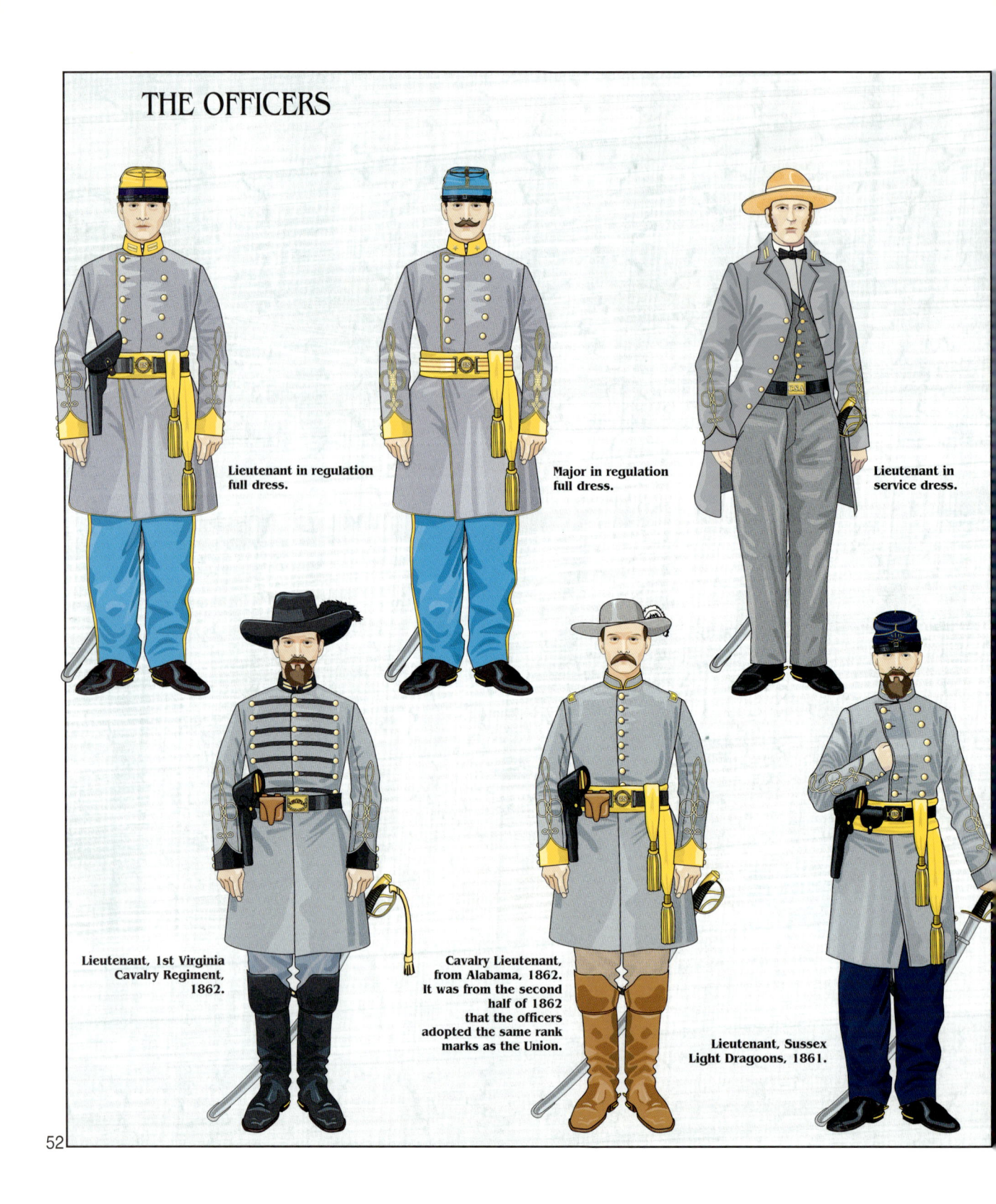

Lieutenant in regulation full dress.

Major in regulation full dress.

Lieutenant in service dress.

Lieutenant, 1st Virginia Cavalry Regiment, 1862.

Cavalry Lieutenant, from Alabama, 1862. It was from the second half of 1862 that the officers adopted the same rank marks as the Union.

Lieutenant, Sussex Light Dragoons, 1861.

52

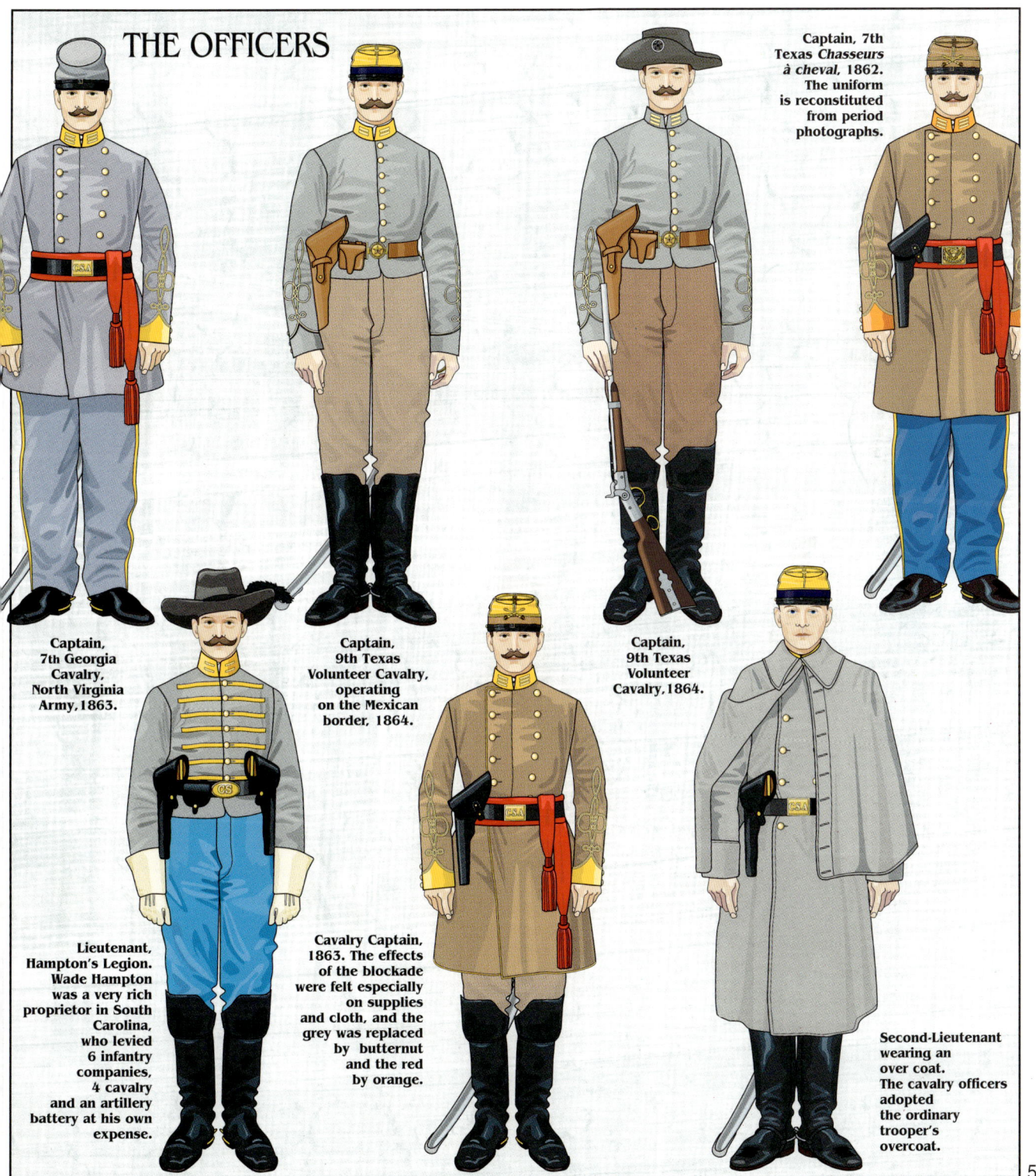

THE OFFICERS

Captain, 7th Texas *Chasseurs à cheval*, 1862. The uniform is reconstituted from period photographs.

Captain, 7th Georgia Cavalry, North Virginia Army, 1863.

Captain, 9th Texas Volunteer Cavalry, operating on the Mexican border, 1864.

Captain, 9th Texas Volunteer Cavalry, 1864.

Lieutenant, Hampton's Legion. Wade Hampton was a very rich proprietor in South Carolina, who levied 6 infantry companies, 4 cavalry and an artillery battery at his own expense.

Cavalry Captain, 1863. The effects of the blockade were felt especially on supplies and cloth, and the grey was replaced by butternut and the red by orange.

Second-Lieutenant wearing an over coat. The cavalry officers adopted the ordinary trooper's overcoat.

53

OFFICERS' EQUIPMENT and DRESS

Service dress regulation cap and forage cap.

General model of a button.

Officer's morning coat, 2nd Maryland Cavalry. The difficulty in finding yellow cloth meant its eventual dissappearance from the uniforms, and even the suppression of the sleeve stripe in certain units.

Major's jacket.

Officer's morning coat, 4th Virginia Cavalry. There were a lot of variations of the grey of the uniforms, from light grey to blue metal grey.

Regulation trousers and waistcoat. The width of the stripe was variable; there was even a double stripe for certain senior officers.

The equipment of the Southern officers was almost identical to that of the North. Small weapons, such as revolvers, were copies of the northern models. However, officers were equipped with weapons imported from England and with individual arms and this gave the cavalry a rather varied appearance.

from top to bottom. Belt buckle. Based on the general model, the belt buckles often represented the different arms or the state symbols for the volunteer units.

54

SADDLERY and EMBLEMS

1st Missouri Cavalry Regiment. This standard was taken by the 11th Wisconsin Infantry Regiment, on 17th May 1863. This unit served at Elkhorn Tavern until its surrender at Vicksburg.

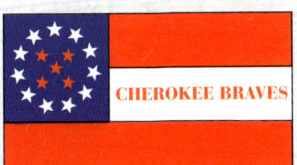

Standard of the 1st Cherokee Cavalry. This unit was composed of Indians recruited in Indian Territory in July 1862. The five red stars represented the five «civilised» tribes: Cherokee, Creek, Chickasaw, Choctaw and Seminole recognised by the Confederates.

1st Arkansas Cavalry Regiment. Dobbin's Regiment was formed in the Spring of 1863 and served in the Missouri expedition in September and October 1864.

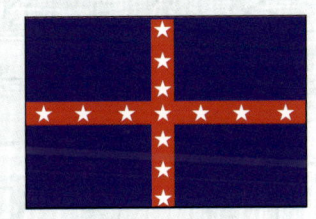

Corporal, Sussex Light dragoons. An integral part of the 5th Virginia, «C» Company was formed in Sussex County. The Dragoons fought in the Army of North Virginia under the command of General Lee. They kept their uniforms up till the end.

Major wearing a jacket with distinctive-coloured lapels. He should be wearing a regulation cap but the majority of the officers wore a black or grey hat.

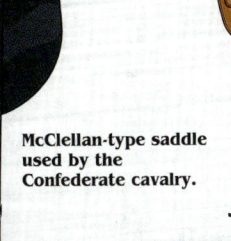

McClellan-type saddle used by the Confederate cavalry.

Officer's saddlebag (non-regulation).

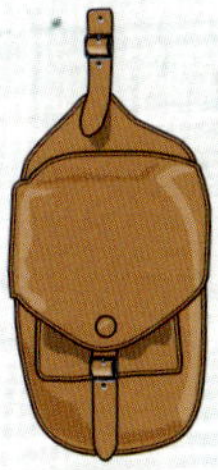

Jenifer-style saddle also used by the Confederate cavalry, made by the C.A. Farwell Company in Mobile, in the State of Alabama.

The CONFEDERATE ARTILLERY

On paper, the organisation was essentially the same as that of the Union. A circular from the War Department of November 1861, fixed the minimum number of men in the companies or batteries at 70, with 10 companies per regiment. This number rose to 150 per company in 1862.

The heavy Artillery was organised in regiments and of the 16 formed, five were from Louisiana, two from North Carolina, three from South Carolina, two from Texas and four from Virginia.

The basic unit of the Light Artillery was the battery, consisting of an average of 4 cannon and 4 horses per artillery train. Often the calibres were not the same. The number of known artillery batteries is between 227 and 261.

Until the winter of 1861, the batteries were assigned to each Brigade Headquarters for the Army of Virginia and for the Army of Tennessee. Towards the spring of 1863, the artillery of the Army of North Virginia was reorganised into battalions. 5 battalions were assigned to an army corps of three divisions which each received a battalion and two in reserve.

The first uniform of the artillerymen was described in the order of 6th June 1861, modified on 24th January 1862, using the grey tunic and red as the distinctive colour of the arm.

During the conflict the uniforms remained standard according to the rule and the artillerymen very quickly adopted the jacket with one row of buttons.

However the uniform varied a lot in quality and colour, sometimes grey, light ochre or even dark ochre, because most part of the uniforms were supplied by the families of the soldiers.

CONFEDERATE ARTILLERY

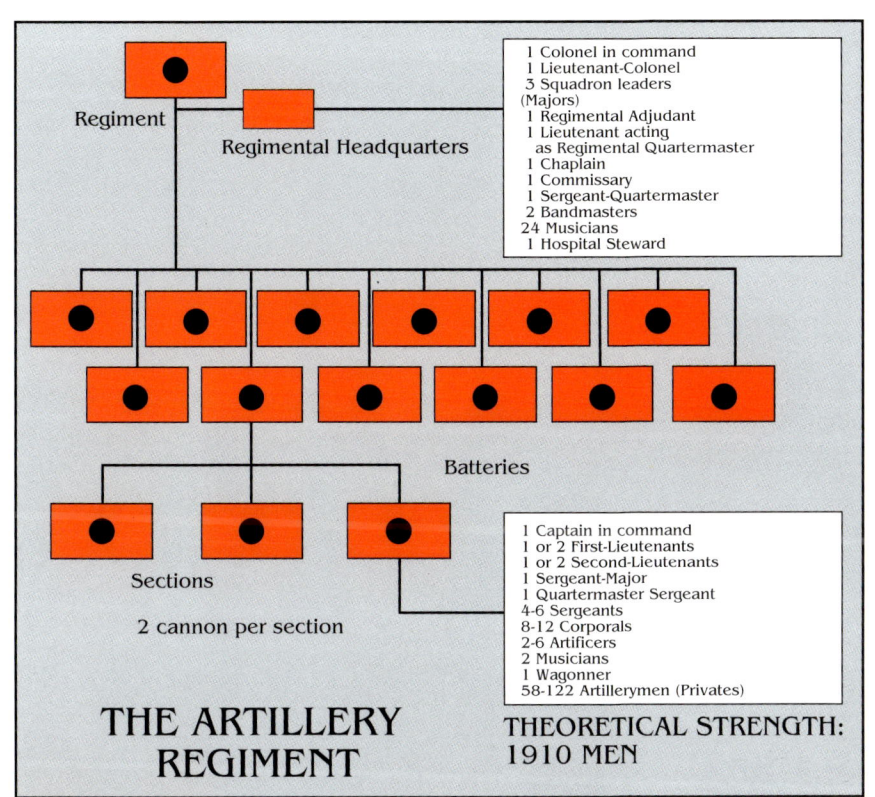

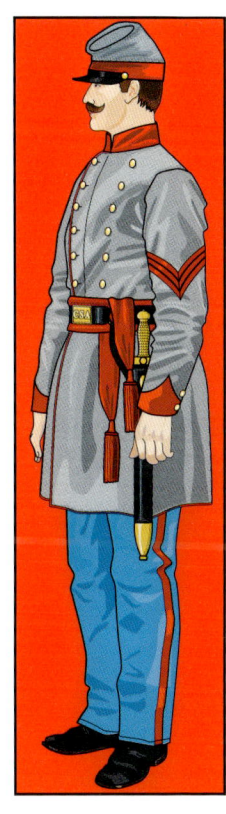

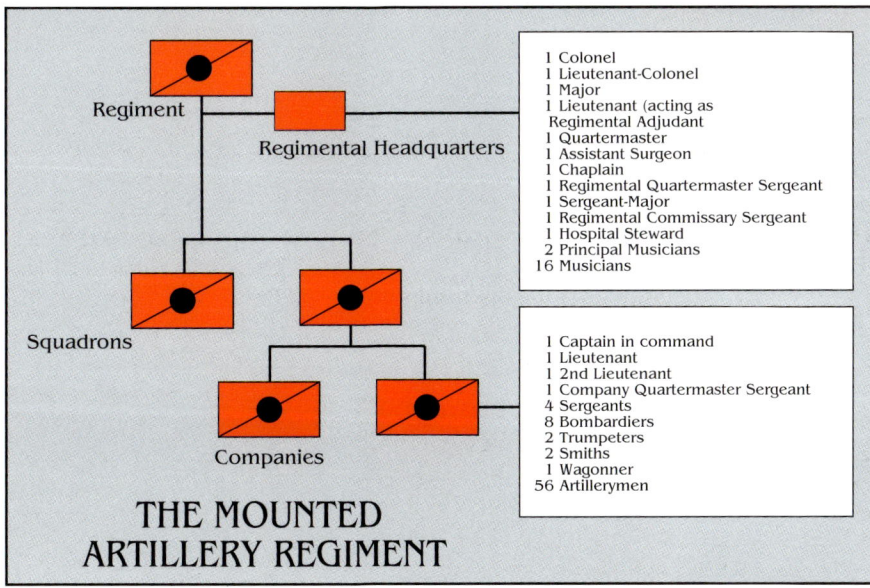

THE ARTILLERY REGIMENT

Regiment — Regimental Headquarters:
- 1 Colonel in command
- 1 Lieutenant-Colonel
- 3 Squadron leaders (Majors)
- 1 Regimental Adjudant
- 1 Lieutenant acting as Regimental Quartermaster
- 1 Chaplain
- 1 Commissary
- 1 Sergeant-Quartermaster
- 2 Bandmasters
- 24 Musicians
- 1 Hospital Steward

Batteries

Sections — 2 cannon per section

- 1 Captain in command
- 1 or 2 First-Lieutenants
- 1 or 2 Second-Lieutenants
- 1 Sergeant-Major
- 1 Quartermaster Sergeant
- 4-6 Sergeants
- 8-12 Corporals
- 2-6 Artificers
- 2 Musicians
- 1 Wagonner
- 58-122 Artillerymen (Privates)

THEORETICAL STRENGTH: 1910 MEN

THE MOUNTED ARTILLERY REGIMENT

Regiment — Regimental Headquarters:
- 1 Colonel
- 1 Lieutenant-Colonel
- 1 Major
- 1 Lieutenant (acting as Regimental Adjudant)
- 1 Quartermaster
- 1 Assistant Surgeon
- 1 Chaplain
- 1 Regimental Quartermaster Sergeant
- 1 Sergeant-Major
- 1 Regimental Commissary Sergeant
- 1 Hospital Steward
- 2 Principal Musicians
- 16 Musicians

Squadrons

Companies:
- 1 Captain in command
- 1 Lieutenant
- 1 2nd Lieutenant
- 1 Company Quartermaster Sergeant
- 4 Sergeants
- 8 Bombardiers
- 2 Trumpeters
- 2 Smiths
- 1 Wagonner
- 56 Artillerymen

THE CONFEDERATE ARTILLERYMAN

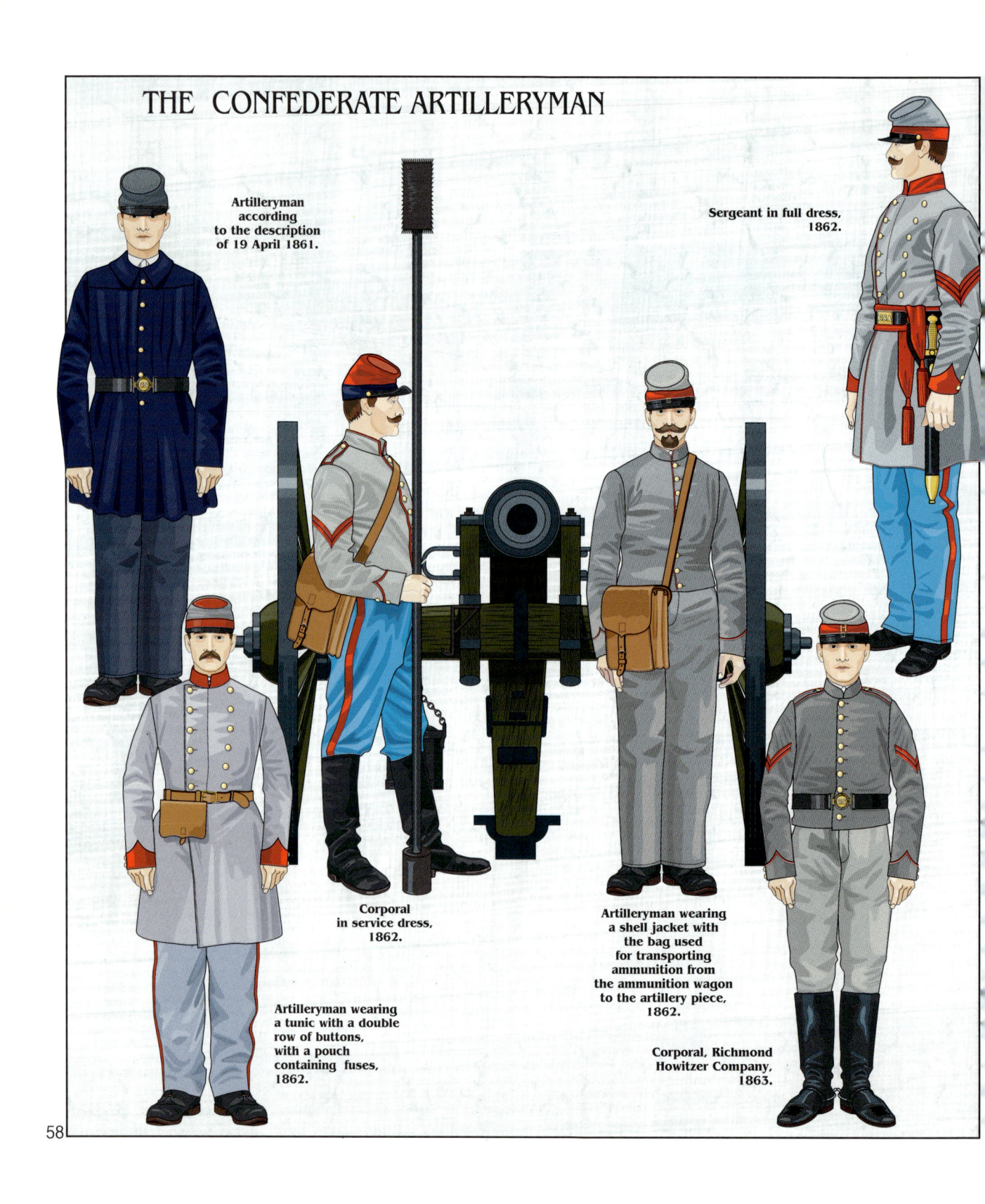

Artilleryman according to the description of 19 April 1861.

Sergeant in full dress, 1862.

Corporal in service dress, 1862.

Artilleryman wearing a tunic with a double row of buttons, with a pouch containing fuses, 1862.

Artilleryman wearing a shell jacket with the bag used for transporting ammunition from the ammunition wagon to the artillery piece, 1862.

Corporal, Richmond Howitzer Company, 1863.

Flag of the 5th Company when this belonged to General Hardee's Corps in 1863.

Washington Light Artillery. Created in 1838 as the «First American battery» («A» Company in Persifal Smith's Regiment), it served in the Mexican War. It was re-organised at New Orleans in 1852 and was entirely composed of ordinary citizens from this town. The artillery corps was composed of 4 companies followed soon after by a fifth, all entirely equipped by the arsenal at Bâton Rouge. It also had 6 six-pounders. Four companies were present at the First Battle of Bull Run, the fifth distinguished itself at Shiloh. Afterwards, the Artillery Corps took part in all the operations of the Army of North Virginia.

From left to right :
Artilleryman in full dress with the «WLA» insignia, 1861.
Artilleryman in service dress, 1862.
Artilleryman in field dress, 1862.

Artilleryman of the Richmond Howitzer Company. He is wearing the artillery sword. Certain soldiers had a belt plate with the arms of the State of Virginia, 1862.

Artilleryman wearing an overcoat, 1st Virginia Regiment. This included a company called the «Richmond Howitzer Company», 1861.

Light artillery soldier wearing an overcoat. The Light Artillery wore the cavalry overcoat whereas the Heavy artillery wore that of the infantry.

59

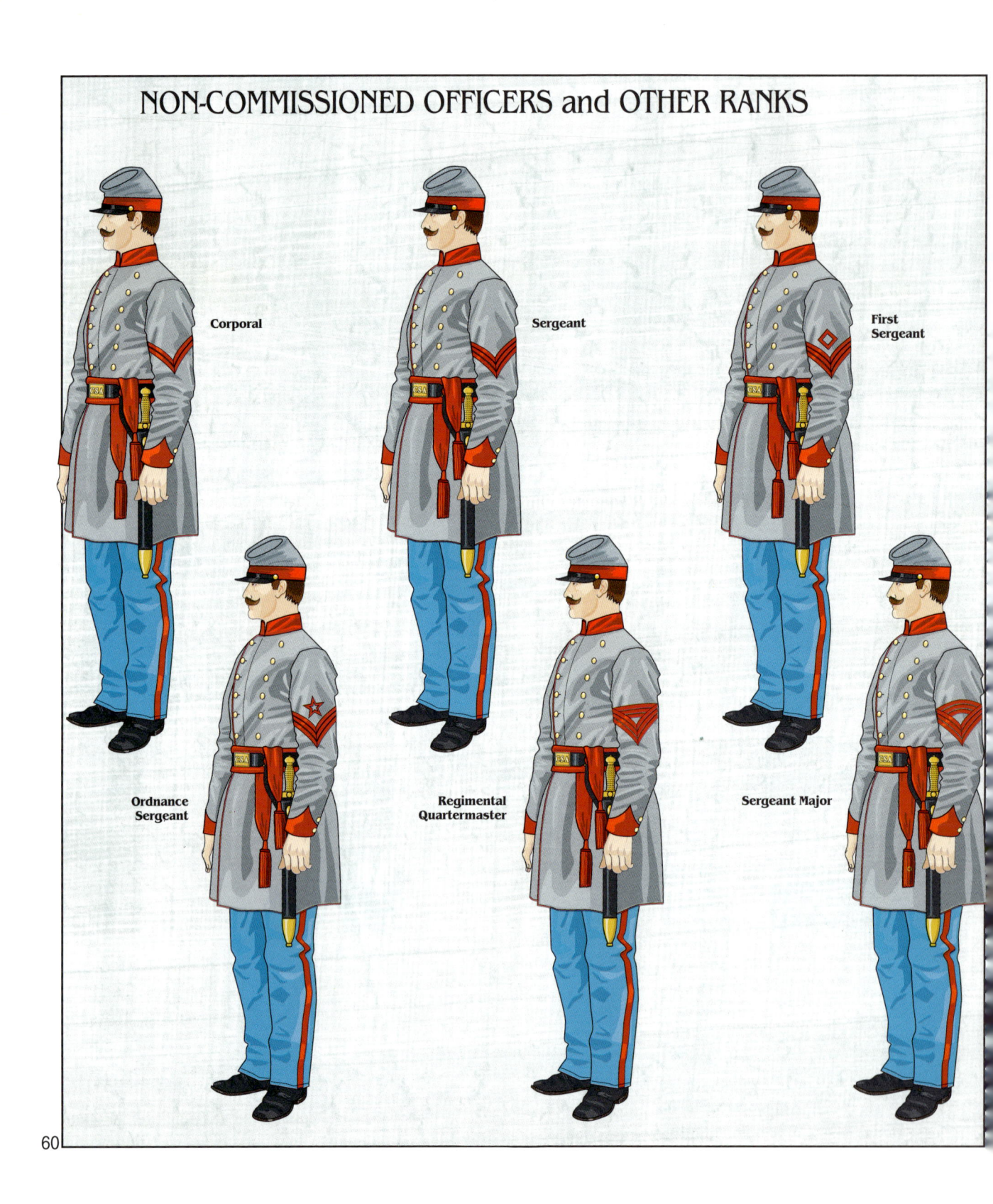

NON-COMMISSIONED OFFICERS and OTHER RANKS

Corporal

Sergeant

First Sergeant

Ordnance Sergeant

Regimental Quartermaster

Sergeant Major

CLOTHING

Full dress cap with the red distinctive with a blue band (Regulation 24 June 1862) and field dress cap (Forage cap). The regulation of 6 June 1861 prescribed a red pompom which seems to have been abandonned very quickly.

Artillery uniform button. Other designs exist especially with the arms of the State.

Shirt. As this was a personal item there were many colors. White and red however were the most common.

Full dress tunic.

Shell jacket and one of its variations made at the Richmond Depot.

With the shortage, braces became simple strips of cloth with 3 or 4 buttonholes.

Waistcoat

Trousers with wide side stripes for the officers. According to the 1862 Regulation, the trousers were sky-blue. Most of the volunteer units wore light grey. As the blockade began to make itself felt, light ochre (butternut) and cloth from Nîmes — de Nîmes = Denim — and Jeans appeared.

Boots.

Example of a mounted-artillery boot. In the Southern States, the majority of soldiers equipped themselves, so there is no one particular model.

61

EQUIPMENT

The Heavy Artilleryman was equipped like the infantryman, and likewise suffered from the supply problem and the disparity of the equipment.

Belt plates of a general model and one from Texas with the Star.

Cap pouches.

NCO's sword, exactly the same as the ones in the Union Army.

Light Artillery equipment with holster and revolver.

Cartridge pouches. Towards the end of the conflict, the different models were made out of cloth strips and painted cloth.

Haversack.

Flasks (*from left to right*) made of wood, metal, and some were rectangular.

Cartridge pouch containing fuses for the cannon.

Haversack made of cloth. It often replaced the Knapsack.

Supply bag for carrying ammunition to the artillery piece

62

CONFEDERATE ARTILLERY OFFICERS

Second-Lieutenant in regulation full dress, 1862.

Lieutenant in service dress, 1862.

Captain in field dress, wearing a cap covered in oiled cloth and painted with the colours of the artillery, 1863.

A group of officers of the Washington Light Artillery coming from New Orleans. The officers wore the same shoulder flaps as the Union artillery officers. Sources show some differences in detail on the facing and how the insignia were worn. The scarf worn over the shoulder shows that this was a duty officer.

The OFFICERS and the ARTILLERYMEN

Lieutenant, Light Artillery, 1864.

Captain, 17th Virginia Light Artillery Battalion, 1863. The uniform has been made up from different items to which grey trousers and a pair of boots have been added.

Captain, 1st Tennessee Light Artillery. The battery of Captain Rutledge was formed in May 1861 at Nashville and became «A» Company, 1st Tennessee Light Artillery.

Artilleryman from Crenshaw's Battery, from the Richmond artillery. On the cap can be seen the artillery insignia and the letters C and B, 1863.

Gunner, 18th Virginia Artillery Regiment 1861-62. The figure has been reconstructed from a period photograph. He has been given a pair of grey trousers together with a cap of the same colour bearing the crossed cannon with, perhaps, the company letter which has not been identified.

Gunner, Lynchburg Artillery Company, 1861. The figure has been realised from the period photograph of a bust. The soldier wears no hat, so he has been given an artillery hat. The black and white photograph makes the stripes on the shirt appear to be darker than they should be; they have been coloured in red since the soldier belongs to the artillery.

The OFFICER'S RANKS

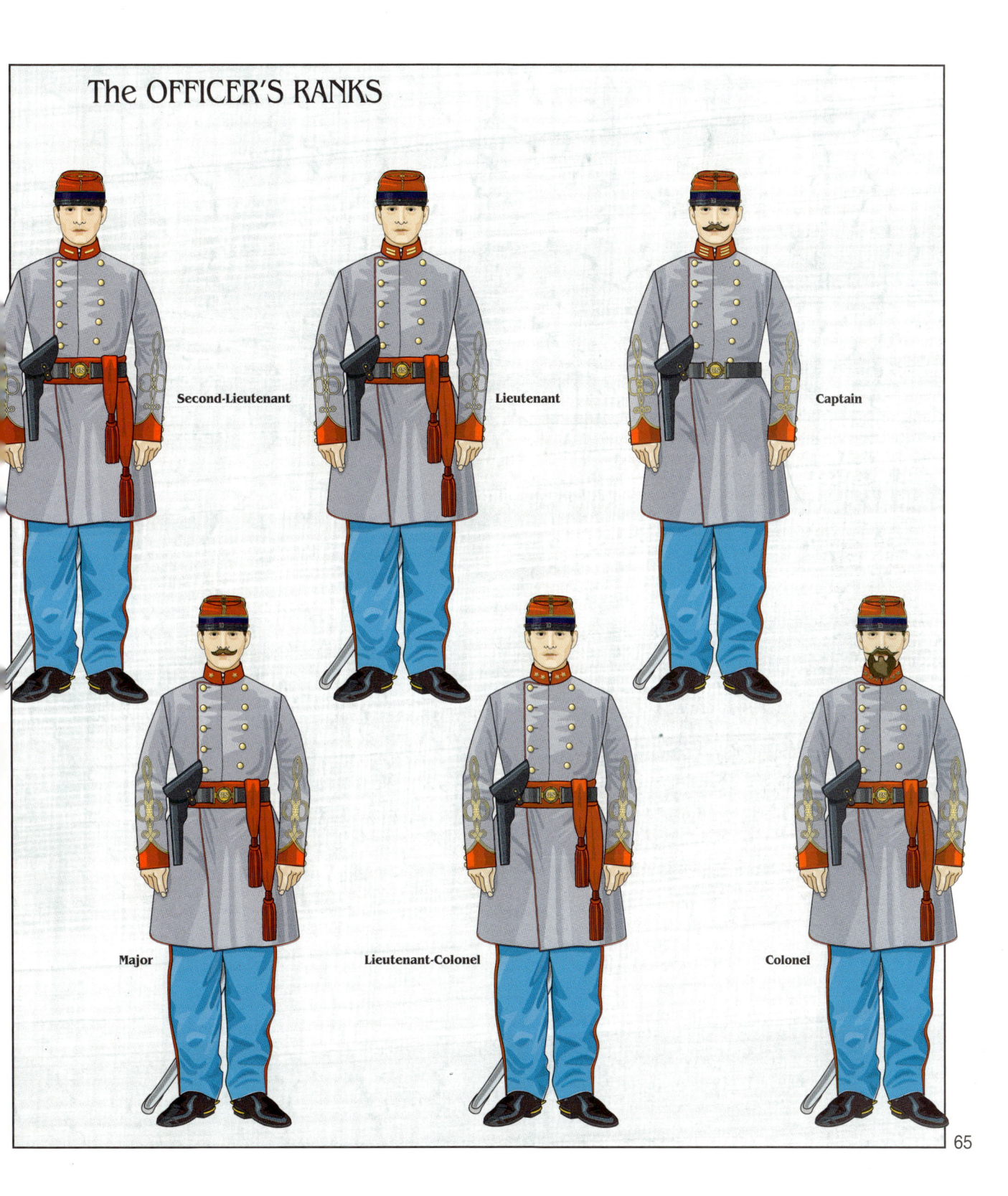

Second-Lieutenant

Lieutenant

Captain

Major

Lieutenant-Colonel

Colonel

EQUIPMENT and DRESS

Uniform button, general model for officers. Artillery buttons.

Lieutenant's *(from above)* **and Captain's** *(from the front)* **regulation caps. Oiled cloth forage cap.**

Captain's shell jacket.

Captain's tunic. For economy's sake, there was no longer any red on the facings nor any knots *à la hongroise.*

Major's jacket Butternut version.

Officer's equipment and weapons.

Waistcoat.

Gloves.

Regulation Trousers.

Field dress bag.

Flasks.

66

EMBLEMS

20th Louisiana Artillery Regiment.

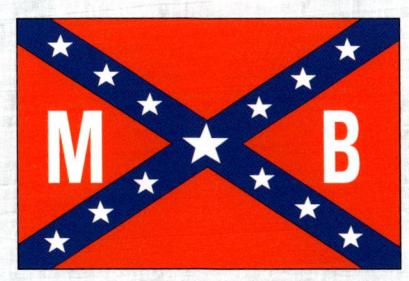

Morton's Battery, Army of North Virginia.

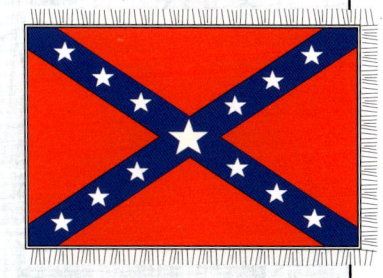

Vernon's Battery, Texas Artillery.

10th North Carolina Volunteer Regiment, «C» Company, 1st Artillery Regiment.

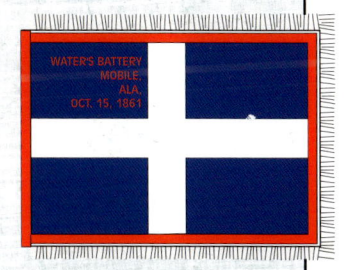

Water's Battery, from the State of Alabama, Army of Tennessee.

Marion's Battery, South Carolina.

18th South Carolina Artillery Regiment, «A» Company, Fort Sumter, 1861

Palmetto's Battery, State of South Carolina. Quartermaster-Sergeant Standard-Bearer, 1864.

67

EQUIPMENT

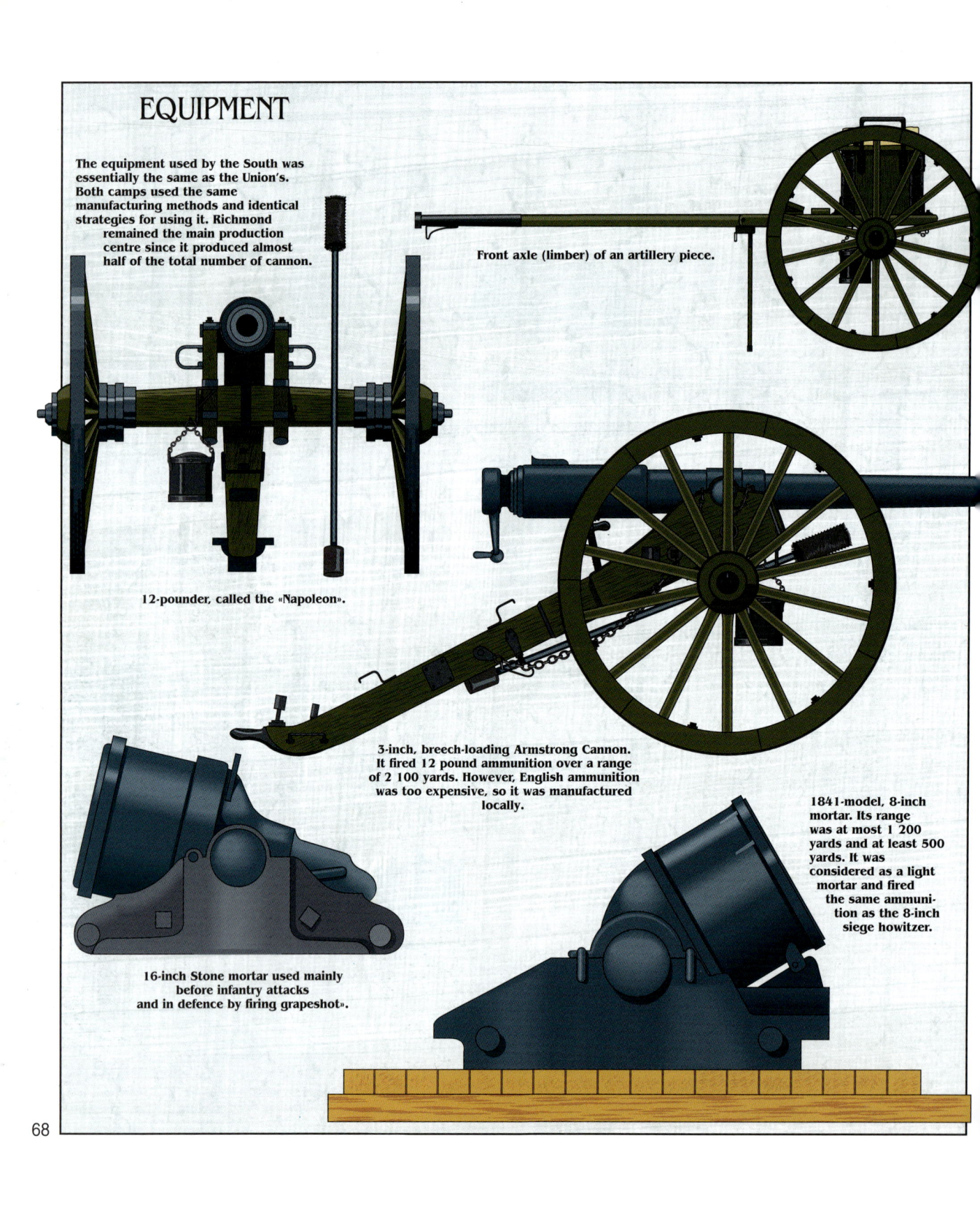

The equipment used by the South was essentially the same as the Union's. Both camps used the same manufacturing methods and identical strategies for using it. Richmond remained the main production centre since it produced almost half of the total number of cannon.

Front axle (limber) of an artillery piece.

12-pounder, called the «Napoleon».

3-inch, breech-loading Armstrong Cannon. It fired 12 pound ammunition over a range of 2 100 yards. However, English ammunition was too expensive, so it was manufactured locally.

16-inch Stone mortar used mainly before infantry attacks and in defence by firing grapeshot».

1841-model, 8-inch mortar. Its range was at most 1 200 yards and at least 500 yards. It was considered as a light mortar and fired the same ammunition as the 8-inch siege howitzer.

68

CONFEDERATE GENERAL OFFICERS

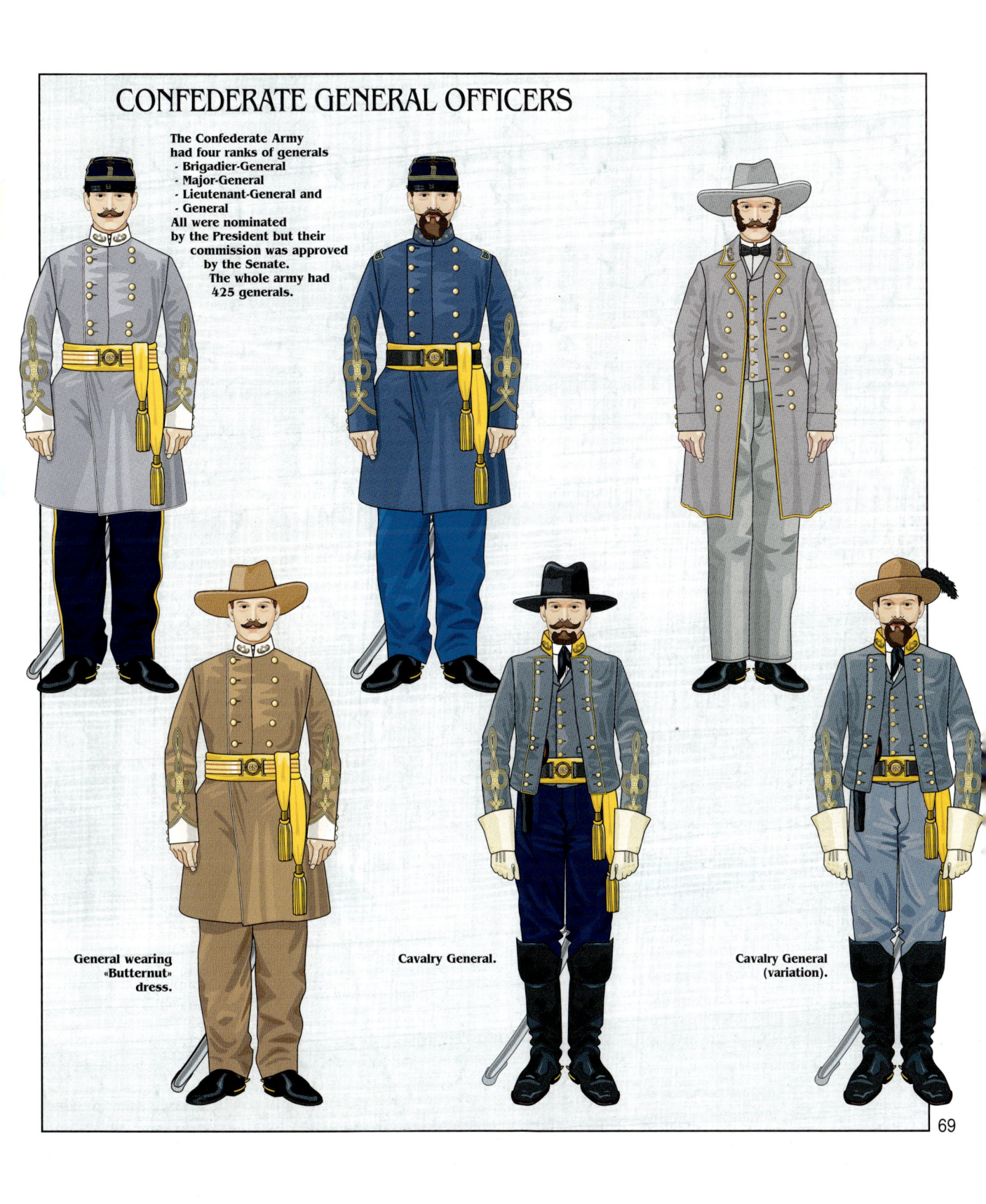

The Confederate Army had four ranks of generals
- Brigadier-General
- Major-General
- Lieutenant-General and
- General

All were nominated by the President but their commission was approved by the Senate. The whole army had 425 generals.

General wearing «Butternut» dress.

Cavalry General.

Cavalry General (variation).

69

The CONFEDERATE ARMY'S SERVICES

THE ENGINEER SERVICE

AT THE BEGINNING THE CORPS WAS MADE UP of non-commissioned officers under the command of the central office of the Engineer Corps and included a company of sappers, miners and bridge makers.

The officers of the Engineer Corps were attached to the Headquarters staff of each Army, Army Corps, Division and Brigade.

Work carried out by the Engineers was done by soldiers taken from the infantry regiments.

The building and the destruction of bridges, works and fortifications were asigned to specialists assisted by infantry elements.

The 1st Battalion of the Engineer Corps was organised by the Trans-Mississippi Department during the winter of 1863-64 into 4 companies, which became the 1st Regiment serving with the Army of North Virginia.

The 2nd Regiment was organised in the summer of 1863, and its companies were spread out among all the theatres of operations of the Confederate army.

The 3rd regiment was created at the same time with 9 companies whereas the 4th only had three.

The officers of the Engineer Corps wore the standard officer's uniform with light ochre distinctives. NCOs wore stripes of the same colour, or white.

THE SIGNALS SERVICE

Before the war, Second-Lieutenant Edward P. Alexander was Captain Myer's assistant in setting up a signalling system based on a system of torches and flags. On the declaration of war, E.P. Alexander joined the Confederate ranks and during the First battle of Bull Run was of considerable help in the signalling of messages and thus contributed to the Confederate victory.

The 1st Signals Corps was created in April 1862. Put under the command of Captain W. Norris, it consisted of 10 junior officers, 10 NCOs with a sufficient number of soldiers. In November of the same year, this was increased to 30 officers and 30 NCO's; a detachment of 3-5 soldiers under the command of an NCO or a lieutenant was affected to each cavalry brigade's or division's headquarters staff. At the same time a second corps was created by a navy officer who operated on the shores of Virginia.

The Army of Tennessee also created a signal service towards the end of 1862. Centralised at Richmond, the Signals Corps were not only responsible for internal communications but also had a military information and counter-espionage bureau.

The signals officers, like the NCOs wore the Engineers' uniform with a signals insignia identical to the Union's but made of silvery metal.

The CONFEDERATE ARMY'S SERVICES

THE MEDICAL SERVICE

As with the Union army, the Medical Service was under the responsability of a Surgeon-General and his staff, consisting of 2 senior assistant officers, one for the Trans-Mississippi department and the other at Richmond, with 5 doctors.

In September 1864, the management of the service comprised :
— 18 surgeon commanders who were spread out among the different army corps,
— 8 Surgeons in command of hospitals,
— 6 Surgeon Inspectors to which were added a variable number of Surgeon-Inspectors per hospital,
— Surgeon-Suppliers and 5 doctors responsible for controlling the medical expertise of the surgeons, all having the rank of Colonel.

All the doctors serving in the field hospitals or the regiments were majors.

About 1 000 doctors served in the Confederate ranks, to which must be added assistants recruited by contract having the rank of Second-Lieutenant. Doctors were considered by the Union and Confederation alike as non-combattants and were not prisoners of war if captured.

The majority of the doctors held a practice in the countryside or in the small towns and were more used to accidents and births than to the serious traumatisms of war casualties. Although medicine of the time did not use anasthetic, the most serious risks were infectious diseases and post-operatory problems.

In the Army of North Virginia, towards mid-1863, the Medical service was organised under a Surgeon-Commander of the Army, with a Surgeon-Commander for each corps and each brigade.

Each regiment had its doctor and his assistant, two ambulances and a sanitary wagon. Two men per company were attached to the Medical Service as stretcher-bearers, followed the troops into combat and evacuated the wounded to the rear and the hospitals.

The regimental musicians were often used for this task.

Each regiment had a hospital steward who had some knowledge of medicine and drugs. He was assisted by an administrator and was responsible for the wounded and their evacuation.

The same personnel was affected to hospitals as well as the nurses, 2 medics and 2 assistants per 100 beds.

The main hospital was Huge Chimborazo in Richmond, consisting of 5 hospitals which could receive 4 800 wounded at any one time.

The ENGINEERS

Uniform buttons. The Gothic «E» is a local fabrication, the emblem of the castle, English.

Major, 1st Engineer Regiment, Army of North Virginia, 1865.

Lieutenant-Colonel in full dress, 1862.

Major in full dress, 1862.

Captain in service dress, 1864.

Chief Engineer A.N.V

Flag of the Engineer Headquarters of the army of North Virginia.

Sergeant, 1st Regiment of Engineers, 1864. He is equipped with a rifle, a spade and a pick.

Major in field dress, 1864.

The SIGNALS CORPS and the MEDICAL SERVICE

Surgeon-Major, 1863, wearing regulation dress. The cap is blue and bears an insignia on a velvet background with the letters M S among laurel leaves. There was no regulation sabre for doctors.

Surgeon-Major, 1864.

Confederate Signals Corps Lieutenant.

Hospital Steward, responsible for the administrative organisation of the field hospital, keeping and managing the medicine supplies. This job was given over to First Sergeants or to Sergeant-Majors.

This pennant indicates the presence of a field hospital and serves as a marking out sign to indicate the first field hospital.

Ambulanceman. These were soldiers detached as stretcher-bearers responsible for evacuating the wounded to the field hospitals. They wore a band on their headgear showing their job.

THE BATTLE OF GETTYSBURG

At the end of May 1863, General Lee's southern army carried the war right into Yankee territory. The primary objective was to force the North to lift the Siege of Vicksburg, but Lee was also prepared to fight a decisive battle which could end the war...

In the Spring of 1863, the Confederation's situation was both good and bad. Indeed, although the Army of Virginia, commanded by Lee. had won a thundering victory at Chancellorville (1st-4th May) over the Army of the Potomac and broken the Union's offensive against Richmond, General Grant had forced his way through to Vicksburg, the southern fortress that controlled the Mississippi, and besieged the town.

The Confederate President, Jefferson Davis, wondered how best to use Lee and his army. It was clear that if the siege of Vicksburg was not lifted, the fortress would be lost at more or less long term. This would give the North total control of the Mississippi. Several choices were possible: send part of the Army of North Virginia, or even better, launch an offensive in Tennessee to force Lincoln to call back Grant.

Moreover the northern Army of the Potomac, still before Richmond, was slowly reforming and would certainly, in the medium term, renew its offensive on the Confederate capital. This army, commanded by Hooker, was slow and the other options could be tried before it would react.

Lee submitted his own plan to President Davis: the invasion of Pennsylvania. According to him, carrying the war into the heart of the Union would force the northern armies to fall back or at least to postpone their operations until the following year. This would permit Virginia to be spared the war during the summer months and the southern army could live off Pennsylvania's rich lands. Lee's objectives were rather limited because unless he won a victory over the whole of the Army of the Potomac and thus seriously threatened Washington, there was little likelihood that the North would stop fighting and that England would finally recognise the Confederation.

ENTERING PENNSYLVANIA

At the end of May, the southern Army of North Virginia was to the south of Rappahannock River, at Fredericksburg; the Army of the Potomac was on the other side of the river. The Army of Virginia was probably the best large unit on both sides. Its commander, General Lee was adored by his men. A reasoned man, but capable of audacious manoeuvres, he was a brilliant strategist.

From the 3rd June, the southern 1st Corps under the command of Longstreet, began to move north-west, followed shortly by Ewell's 2nd Corps, with Stuart's cavalry making a screen at Brandy Station. Hill's 3rd Corps remained behind. the Army of Virginia moved towards The Shenandoah Valley, from which it could move rapidly towards the north, unseen by the northern reconnaissance. In front, Hooker, wanting to know where Ewell was, sent Pleasanton and his cavalry off on reconnaissance. They surprised Stuart at Brandy Station on 9th June: the cavalry battle which followed was the biggest of the conflict, but neither side obtained a decisive victory.

Hooker began manoeuvering parallel with Lee, and sent Reynolds with the 1st, 3rd, 5th and 11th Corps ahead towards Manassas. On the 14th, Ewell took Winchester and routed the garrison which fled towards Harper's Ferry. The last corps of the Army of Virginia, Hill's, left Fredericksburg to join the rest of the army.

On the 22nd June, Lee, knowing that Hooker was pursuing him, began to get his army across the Potomac. While Hill's and Longstreet's corps were concentrating at Chambersburg, Ewell was marching to the north-east towards the Susquehanna River. The 25th June, Stuart on his way for a raid around the Army of the Potomac, just avoided Hancock's 2nd Corps and was obliged to find a way across the Potomac further east, which the North's foremost units had already reached. One wing, under the command of Reynolds, crossed at Edwards Ferry. On 28th June, General Meade took command of the Army of the Potomac, relieving Hooker.

At the end of June, Lee's three corps followed each other, spread out over a large arc of more than 30 miles. Lee learnt through a spy that the Army of the Potomac was already in Maryland. The following day, he decided to recall Ewell and to concentrate the army towards Cashtown. Because he was a manoeuvrer, he wanted to get the Army of the Potomac into a big battle and destroy it. He thought that it would not have sufficient time to concentrate. On the 30th, Ewell's divisions regrouped before moving towards Gettysburg. The rest of the army was still at Cashtown. In the northern camp, Buford's cavalry division, on a reconnaissance mission, penetrated into Gettysburg; the rest of the army of the Potomac was advancing slowly northwards. Neither Meade nor Lee expected to encounter the other in the next 24 hours. On the evening of this same 30th June, Hill authorised one of his divisions to enter Gettysburg for requisitioning purposes. If the South's headquarters were aware of the presence of Northern cavalry, they believed the Army of the Potomac to be at Middleburg, more to the south. What began as a simple skirmish very rapidly changed into a decisive clash.

THE BATTLE OF GETTYSBURG.

On the morning of 1st July, Heth's division which was heading towards Gettysburg, stumbled upon Buford's cavalry and made it retreat to McPherson Ridge, before being itself pushed back. Marching to the sound of the cannon, Ewell's divisions hurried one after the other to the place where the fighting had begun. Ewell and Hill gradually pushed the North's 1st Corps towards Seminary Ridge then Cemetery Hill, causing 60% casualties. The northern 11th Corps also collapsed and fell back on Cemetery Hill.

The first day was a success for the southeners: the two armies, surprised at meeting each other, collided head on and it was the North which retreated. His leading corps seriously mauled, Hancock who had taken command, reorganised the northern battle lines with elements of the 3rd and 12th Corps.

Despite his wish to breach the enemy positions with a last attack, Lee did not launch any other actions of any consequence; rather he took advantage of his position to concentrate his army. Victory seemed near for the Confederates: two northern corps had practically disappeared under the assaults of four southern divisions and the Army of the Potomac had still not concentrated.

Unfortunately, the absence of Stuart and his cavalry prevented the the follow-up pursuit and the following morning Lee did not have the necessary information for a full appreciation of the enemy's position. Moreover, generals like Ewell and Hill, brilliant divisional commanders though they were, turned out to be unsatisfactory corps commanders, incapable of leading perfectly coordinated attacks. The absence of «Stonewall» Jackson, who had died as a result of his wounds at the battle of Chancellorsville, was cruelly felt.

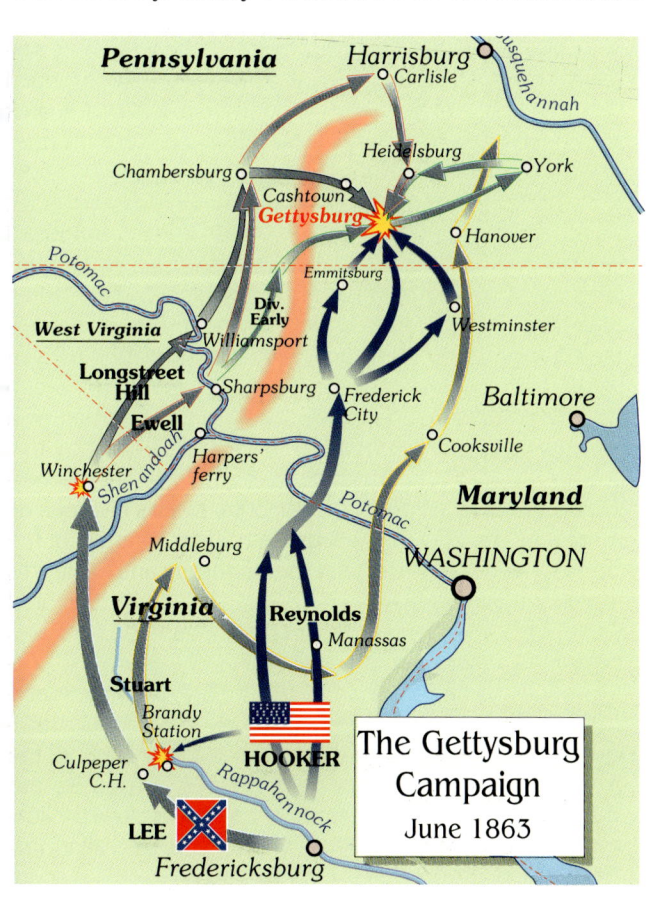

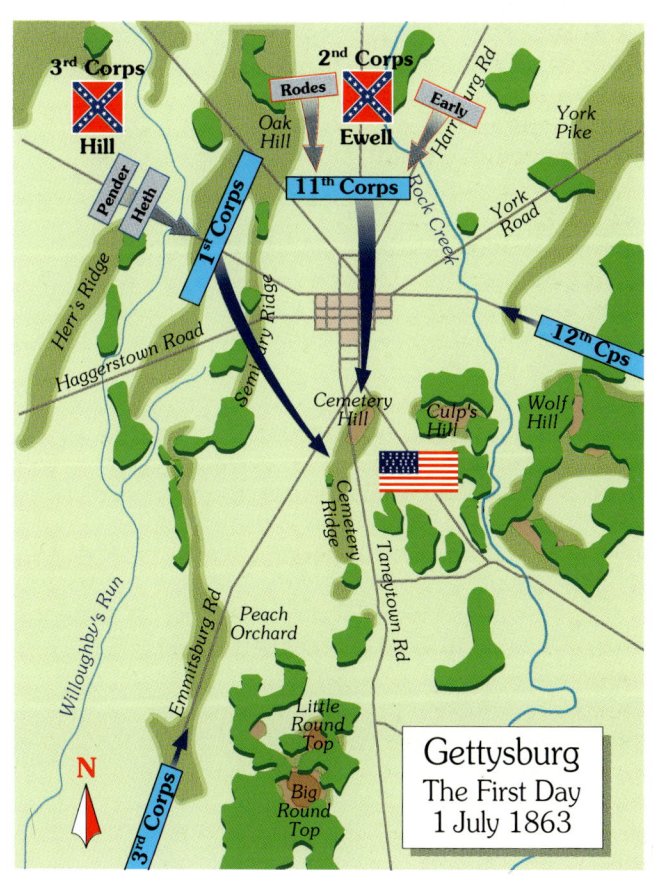

On the 2nd July, the combined attacks of Longstreet and Ewell on the flanks of northern battle line failed. The southern attacks did not succeed in dislodging the Northerners from their excellent defensive positions, anchored in the wooded hills of Little Round Top and Culp Hill. The following day, in a final effort to carry the day, Lee sent Pickett's division, supported by two divisions of Hill's corps to assault the North's centre. 15 000 men supported by 140 cannon - the largest artillery concentration of the war - launched an assault on Cemetery Ridge. The elite of the southern army came to die under the withering fire of the enemy. Only Armistead's Virginian Brigade managed to reach the North's lines and push back the defenders, only to be wiped out by a counter attack. The campaign finished with a grave defeat for the South. In order to save his bloodied army, Lee was obliged to retreat towards Virginia, going back across the Potomac. Meade, happy at having won such a victory, albeit a defensive one, did not risk taking any follow-up advantage and contented himself with following the Army of Virginia at a distance, waiting for a opportunity to attack it. The 13th July, Lee finally crossed the Potomac again at Williamsport, after having been delayed by the river in spate, on the eve of the original attack planned by Meade.

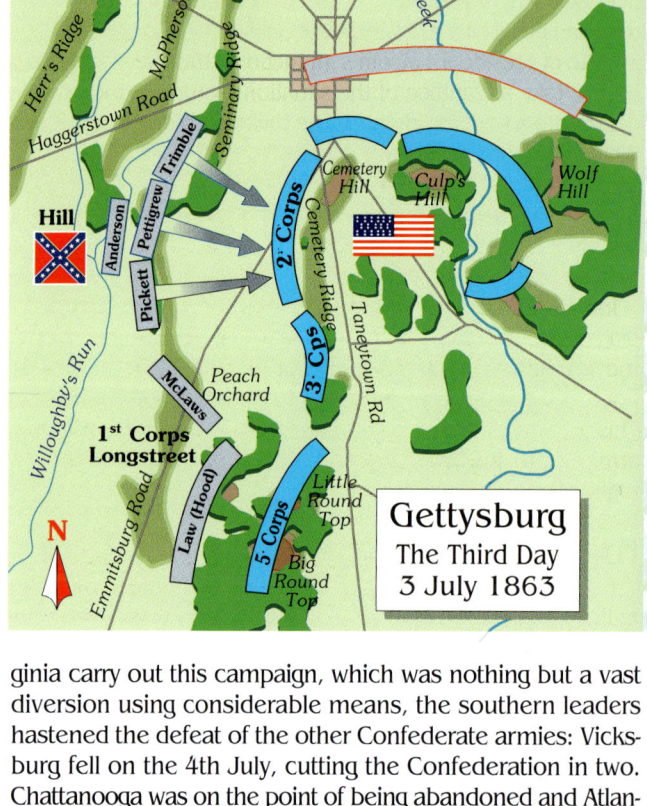

A VICTORY OUT OF REACH.

Lee's defeat at Gettysburg sounded the death knell for the South's hopes of regaining the initiative. From the beginning, the whole of the South's strategy seemed not to have been adapted to circumstances. Indeed, by letting the Army of Virginia carry out this campaign, which was nothing but a vast diversion using considerable means, the southern leaders hastened the defeat of the other Confederate armies: Vicksburg fell on the 4th July, cutting the Confederation in two. Chattanooga was on the point of being abandoned and Atlanta was threatened. By penetrating the North, Lee did oblige the Army of the Potomac to follow him, but Grant's army, getting all the re-inforcements it needed, was able to continue the siege of Vicksburg. Lee's threat to Washington did not really affect the North's strategy.

The risk taken by Lee in engaging the enemy in battle imposed enormous constraints on the South which did not really have the means. At Gettysburg, the losses on both sides were more or less the same, about 28 000 for the South, 23 000 for the Nort; the South was unable to recover from this, whereas the North, in comparison, had endless ressources to draw on. From this point of view, only a brilliant victory, which was almost impossible to achieve when one strong army confronted another such as at Gettysburg, would have changed the outcome of the conflict.

Nicolas Stratigos

The Battle of CHICKAMAUGA

At the end of the summer 1863, the situation on all fronts of the Civil War was a paroxysm of paradoxes. The feeling that the outcome of the war could be definitively favourable to the North was almost shared by everybody. It only needed a little more... In fact, Meade and the Army of the Potomac had inflicted a historic defeat on Lee and his generals but, in spite of President Lincoln's injunctions, they had not known how to take advantage of the situation by turning the South's defeat into a rout. In Arkansas, the Union General Blunt with his White, Black and Indian regiments, after a lot of mishaps, managed to capture Fort Smith in the first days of September 1863. A northern army coming west in support of his campaign penetrated Little Rock on 10th September. One of the Old South's bastions in the west of the country had just fallen to the North.

In Tennessee, the northern General Rosencrans, commanding the Army of the Cumberland, was ordered to imitate Grant's movements in the Mississppi in order to put pressure on all fronts at the same time, according to President Lincoln's wishes. This was the only strategy which would prevent the southern armies from supporting and re-inforcing each other and countering the Yankee offensives.

Fortunes and misfortunes of being too careful

But Rosencrans, perhaps more humane than his peers or, rather, traumatised by the bloody campaign of Stones River, the preceding winter, did not want to advance before having regrouped all the forces necessary, if not indispensible, for a real victory. What passed at best for procrastination in the eyes of the Union General Staff enabled Confederate General Bragg to send units of his Army of Tennessee in support of the southern Army of Mississippi in the Spring of 1863. But Rosencrans' tactics were sound as the beginning of his campaign on 24th June proved. In one week, losing only 570 men, Rosencrans and his five corps (four infantry and one cavalry) cut the lines of communication and supply of his adversary Bragg and made him retreat 80 miles, driving him back on Chattanooga, the most important railway junction of the southern forces and the primary objective of the Army of the Cumberland's campaign.

This tactical success, justly considered by the southern generals as a master stroke was totally overshadowed by Meade's victory at Gettysburg and the fall of Vicksburg.

The general himself retorted to the Ministry of War with these scarcely amenable words: «*In its name, I beg the Ministry of War not to neglect such a great event because it has not been written in letters of blood*». Which says a lot for the attitude of general officers concerning casualties and the value of success on the battlefield. The rest of the campaign conformed more to the usual customs and methods of the time. It remains that Rosencrans' penetration left Chattanooga and its railroads, and Knoxville, the centre of the North's partisans in this southern-state, within reach. Chattanooga was the gateway to Georgia. Its capture would imply cutting up the Confederate territory yet further, after the split following the fall of Vicksburg, but this time it would be on the eastern side. The opportunity was too good for the North's strategists to miss: Burnside on the west with the army of Ohio, was to head for Knoxville and the Army of the Cumberland, the bigger force, was to take Chattanooga.

If Burnside, coming from Kentucky, set off immediately, Rosencrans, true to form, delayed the start of his campaign, wanting to organise his supply and communication lines before penetrating into the heart of enemy territory. These were realistic and careful tactics which did not please Washington. On 16th August 1863, Rosencrans set off towards the south of Chattanooga, with the intention of cutting the railways in the direction of Atlanta. Sixty thousand men in three columns, taking advantage of the natural river passages between the mountains of the Cumberland with, parallel-wise, Burnside's four columns totalling 24 000 men progressed towards Knoxville.

The Battle of Chickamauga River

The southerners, considering that they were caught in a vice between the Unionists at Knoxville and the Army of Ohio, evacuated the town. The Union troops took Knoxville without firing a single shot. Burnside only had to patrol from there to the borders of North Carolina and Virginia to get his hands on the whole of the east of Tennessee. The retreating southern division rejoined the forces of the Army of Tennessee, still under the command of Bragg, who was evacuating Chattanooga so that Rosencrans would not catch him in the town between the river and the mountains. The north of Georgia seemed more suitable for a fight. Psychologically and strategically, the South had not been faced with such a grave crisis since the beginning of 1862. Lee did not want to help Bragg and even stopped Longstreet who had volunteered, from rejoining him. Only the intervention of President Jefferson enabled Longstreet to reinforce Bragg's army. The 850 miles by train across three states for Longstreet's 12 000 men was an Odyssey in itself and only half of them arrived in time for the battle. Learning of this movement, Rosencrans went over to the attack hoping to defeat the enemy before the two southern forces met.

Deceived by false deserters from the South, the Union general advanced quickly into the successive traps laid by Bragg, who unfortunately for him, was badly backed up by the gene-

THE CAMPAIGN

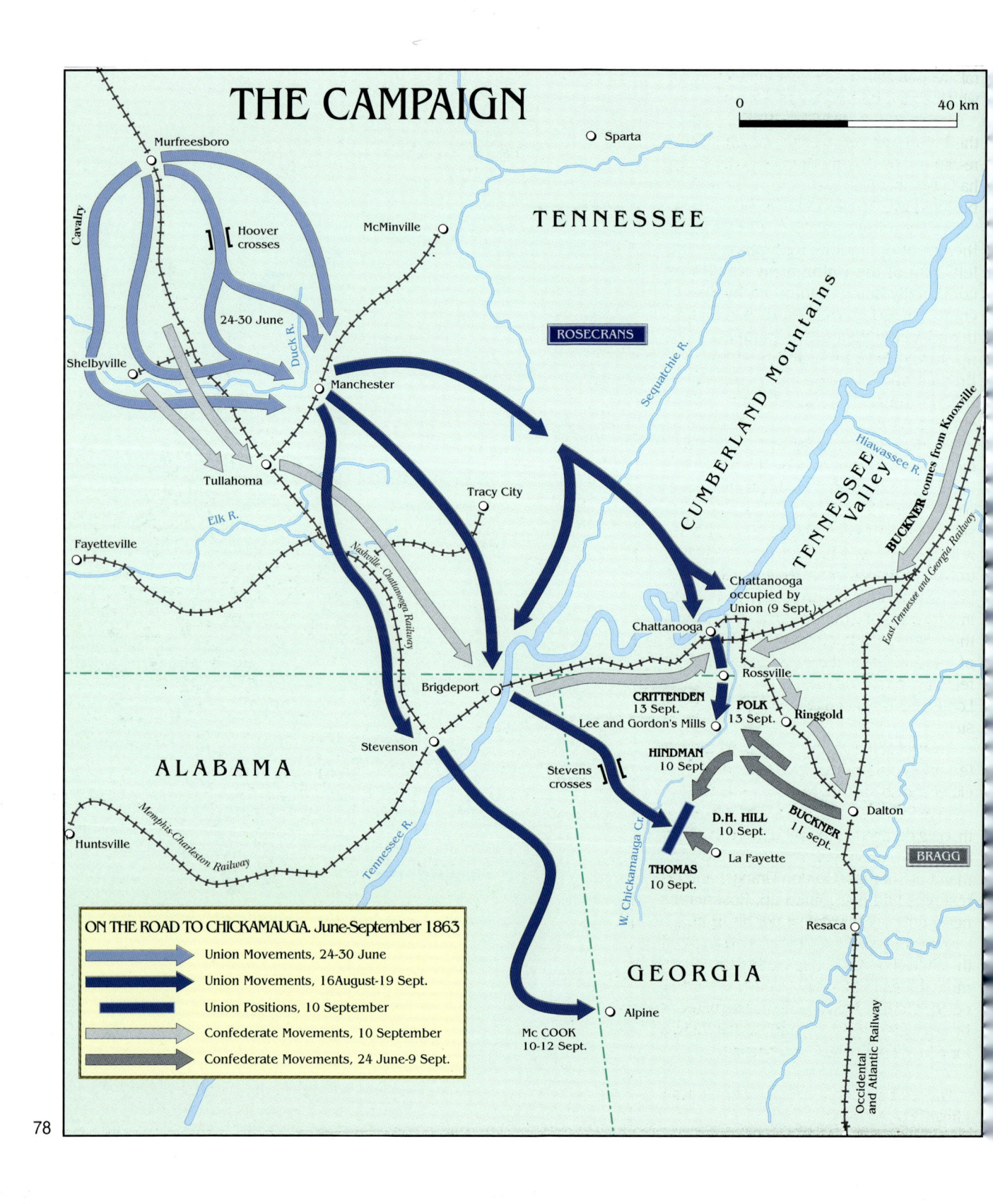

ON THE ROAD TO CHICKAMAUGA, June–September 1863

- Union Movements, 24-30 June
- Union Movements, 16 August-19 Sept.
- Union Positions, 10 September
- Confederate Movements, 10 September
- Confederate Movements, 24 June-9 Sept.

rals responsible for the first three charges, which ended up simply as skirmishes.

On the 19th September, the left wing of the Union was very weak and was quickly re-inforced by General Thomas' corps; Bragg had just missed an easy victory. The serious business was just about to begin.

The bloodiest battle of the western theatre of operations took place on the left wing of the Union army which was continually being re-inforced by Rosencrans. The northern infantry held on tooth and nail to their bits of parapets, built up during the night, and pushed back Bragg's successive assaults. Furious, Bragg ordered Longstreet's men into a single assault.

This fiery general, unawares, took advantage of a terrible mistake on the part of the northern command. Thinking he was stopping a breach in his line of defence (the division holding this part of the line was actually hidden by a wood), Rosencrans removed troops from another part to cover this. That part was where Longstreet's men flooded in, overwhelming the Yankee flanks, making them panic and forcing a third of the Army of the Cumberland's headquarter staff to retreat in a few minutes. Short of reserves, Longstreet was not able to follow up in pursuit.

The right of the southern army was exhausted and could not pursue the advantage either and so the Union troops were able twice to re-form new defensive lines to the north, outside Chattanooga and mix exhausted troops with fresh reserves, under the command of Thomas. Gordon Granger and his reserves had just joined up. Rosencrans never got over this defeat nor his flight.

Longstreet and Forrest wanted to finish off the attack but Bragg, appalled by the loss of more than 20 000 men, killed or wounded, decided to try to reduce the northern troops by starvation, a decision for which he was for a long time bitterly reproached.

The battle for Chattanooga could now effectively start.

Jean-Marie Mongin

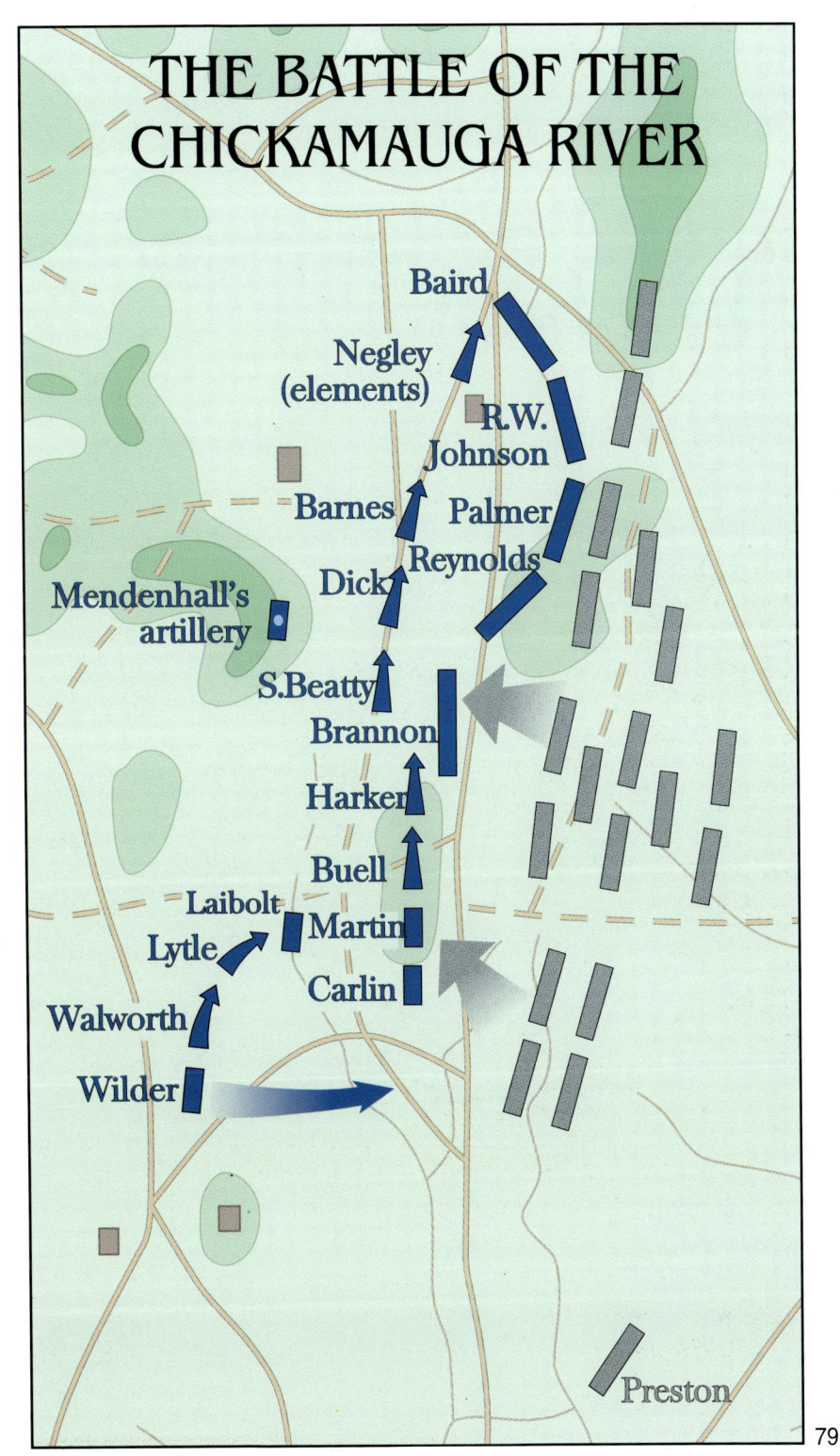

THE BATTLE OF THE CHICKAMAUGA RIVER

ARMY OF CUMBERLAND - UNION

XIV ARMY CORPS
Major General George H. Thomas
9th Michigan Infantry *(Provost Guards)*
1st Ohio Cavalry, *Company L (escort)*

1st Division
Brigadier General Absalom Baird
1st Brigade
Colonel Benjamin F. Scribner
— 38th Indiana
— 2nd Ohio
— 33rd Ohio
— 94th Ohio
— 10th Wisconsin
— 1st Michigan Light Artillery, *Battery A*
2nd Brigade
Brig. General John C. Starkweather
— 24th Illinois
— 79th Pensylvania
— 1st Wisconsin
— 21st Winsconsin
— Indiana Light Artillery, *4th Btty*
3rd Brigade
Brigadier General John H. King
— 15th United States, 1st Battalion
— 16th United States, 1st Battalion
— 18th United States, 1st Battalion
— 18th United States, 2nd Battalion
— 19th United States, 1st Battalion
— 5th US Artillery, *Battery H*

2nd Division
Major General James S. Negley
1st Brigade
Brig Gen John Beatty
— 104th Illinois
— 42nd Indiana
— 88th Indiana
— 15th Kentucky Bridges' *Illinois Btty*
2nd Brigade
Col Timothy R. Stanley
— 37th Indiana
— 21st Ohio
— 74th Ohio
— 78th Pensylvania

3rd Division
Brigadier General John M. Brannan
1st Brigade
Colonel John M. Connell
— 82nd Indiana
— 17th Ohio
— 31st Ohio
— 1st Michigan Light Artillery, *Battery D*
2nd Brigade
Colonel John D. Croxton
Colonel William H. Hays
— 10th Indiana
— 14th Indiana
— 4th Kentucky
— 10th Kentucky
— 14th Ohio
— 1st Ohio Light Artillery, *Battery C*
3rd Brigade
Colonel Ferdinand Van Derveer
— 87th Indianan
— 2nd Minnesota
— 9th Ohio
— 35th Ohio
— 4th US Artillery, *Battery I*

4th Division
Major General Joseph J. Reynolds
1st Brigade
Col John T. Wilder
— 92nd Illinois *(mounted infantry, detached)*
— 98th Illinois
— 123rd Illinois
— 17th Indiana
— 72nd Indiana
— Indiana Light Artillery, *19th Battery*
3rd Brigade
Brigadier General John B. Turchin
— 18th Kentucky
— 11th Ohio
— 36th Ohio
— 92nd Ohio
— Indiana Light Artillery, *21st Battery*

XX ARMY CORPS
Major Gen. Alexander McD. Mc Cook
81st Indiana Infantry, Company H *(Provost Guards)*
2nd Kentucky Cavalry, Company I *(escort)*

1st Division
Brigadier General Jefferson C. Davis
2nd Brigade
Brigadier General William P. Carlin
— 21st Illinois
— 38th Illinois
— 81st Indiana
— 101st Ohio
3rd Brigade
Colonel Hans C. Heg
— 25th Illinois
— 35th Illinois
— 8th Kansas
— 15th Wisconsin
Artillery
Captain William A. Hotchkiss
— Minnesota Light, *2nd Battery*

2nd Division
Brigadier General August Willich
— 89th Illinois
— 32nd Indiana
— 39th Indiana *(mounted infantry, detached)*
— 15th Ohio
— 49th Ohio
— 1st Ohio Light Artillery, *Battery A*

3rd Division
Major General Philip H. Sheridan
1st Brigade
Brigadier General William H. Lytle
Colonel Silas Miller
— 36th Illinois
— 88th Illinois
— 21st Michigan
— 24th Wisconsin
— Indiana Light Artillery, *11th Battery*
2nd Brigade
Colonel Bernard Laiboldt
— 44th Illinois
— 73rd Illinois
— 2nd Missouri
— 15th Missouri
— 1st Missouri Light Artillery, *Battery G*
3rd Brigade
Colonel Luther P. Bradley
Colonel Nathan H. Walworth
— 22nd Illinois
— 27th Illinois
— 42nd Illinois
— 51st Illinois
— 1st Illinois Light Artillery, *Battery C*

XXI ARMY CORPS
Major General Thomas L. Crittenden

1st Division
Brig Gen Thomas J. Wood
1st Brigade
Col George P. Buell
— 100th Illinois
— 58th Indiana
— 26th Ohio
— 13th Michigan
3rd Brigade
Colonel Charles G. Harker
— 3rd Kentucky
— 64th Ohio
— 65th Ohio
— 125th Ohio
Artillery
— Indiana Light, *8th Battery*
— Ohio Light, *6th Battery*

2nd Division
Major General John M. Palmer
1st Brigade
Brigadier General Charles Cruft
— 31st Indiana
— 1st Kentucky *(battalion)*
— 2nd Kentucky
— 90th Ohio
2nd Brigade
Brigadier General William B. Hazen
— 9th Indiana
— 6th Kentucky
— 41st Ohio
— 124th Ohio
3rd Brigade
Colonel William Grose
— 84th Illinois
— 36th Indiana
— 23rd Kentucky
— 6th Ohio
— 24th Ohio
Artillery
Captain William E. Standart
— 1st Ohio Loght, *Battery B*
— 1st Ohio Light, *Battery F*
— 4th United States, *Battery H*
— 4th United States, *Battery M*

3rd Division
Brigadier General Horatio P. Van Cleve
1st Brigade
Brigadier General Samuel Beatty
— 79th Indiana
— 9th Kentucky
— 17th Kentucky
— 19th Ohio
2nd Brigade
Colonel George F. Dick
— 44th Indiana
— 86th Indiana
— 13th Ohio
— 59th Ohio
3rd Brigade
Colonel Sidney M. Barnes
— 35th Indiana
— 8th Kentucky
— 51st Ohio
— 99th Ohio
Artillery
— Indiana Light, *7th Battery*
— Pensylvania Light, *26th Battery*
— Winsconsin Light, *3rd Battery*

RESERVE CORPS
Major General Gordon Granger

1st Division
Brigadier General James B. Steedman
1st Brigade
Brigadier General Walter C. Whitaker
— 96th Illinois
— 115th Illinois
— 84th Indian
— 22nd Michigan
— 40th Ohio
— 89th Ohio
— Ohio Light Artillery, *18th Battery*
2nd Brigade
Colonel John G. Mitchell
— 78th Illinois
— 98th Ohio
— 113th Ohio
— 121st Ohio
— 1st Illinois Light Artillery, *Battery M*

2nd Division
2nd Brigade
Col Daniel McCook
— 85th Illinois
— 86th Illinois
— 125th Illinois
— 52nd Ohio
— 69th Ohio
— 2nd Illinois Light Artillery, *Battery I*

ARMY OF TENNESSEE
General Braxton Bragg
Dreux's Company, Louisiana Cavalry
Holloway's Company, Alabama Cavalry
(General Headquarters' escort)

RIGHT WING
Lieutenant General Leonidas Polk
(Greenleaf's Company, Louisiana Cavalry, (escort)

Cheatham's Division
Major General Benjamin F. Cheatham
(Company G, 2nd Georgia Cavalry , (escort))
Jackson's Brigade
Brigadier General Preston Smith
Colonel Alfred J. Vaughan Jr.
— 11th Tennessee
— 12th Tennessee
— 47th Tennessee
— 13th Tennessee
— 154th Tennessee
— 29th Tennessee
— Dawson's *Sharpshooters*
Maney's Brigade
Brigadier General George Maney
— 1st Tennessee
— 27th Tennessee
— 4th Tennessee *(Provisional Army)*
— 6th Tennessee
— 9th Tennessee
— 24th Tennessee Btn *Sharpshooters*
Wright's Brigade
Brigadier Ben Marcus J. Wright
— 8th Tennessee
— 16th Tennessee
— 28th Tennessee
— 38th Tennessee
— 51st Tennessee
— 52nd Tennessee
Strah's Brigade
Brig Gen Otho F. Strahl
— 4th Tennessee
— 5th Tennessee
— 19th Tennessee
— 24th Tennessee
— 31st Tennessee
— 33rd Tennessee
Artillery
Maj Melanchon Smith
— Carne's (Tennessee) Battery
— Scogin's (Georgia) Battery
— Scott's (Tennessee) Battery
— Smith's (Mississippi) Battery
— Standford's (Mississippi) Battery

RESERVE CORPS
Major General William H. T. Walker

Walker's Division
Brigadier General States R. Gist
Gist's Brigade
Brigadier General States R. Gist
Colonel Peyton JH. Colquitt
Lieutenant-Colonel Leroy Napier
— 46th Georgia
— 8th Georgia Battalion
— 24th South Carolina
Ector's Brigade
Brig Gen Matthew D. Ector
— Stone's (Alabama) Battalion *Sharpshooters*
— Pound's (Mississippi) Battalion *Sharpshooters*
— 29th North Carolina
— 9th Texas
— 10th Texas Cavalry
— 14th Texas Cavalry
— 12th Texas Cavalry
Wilson's Brigade
Colonel Claudius C. Wilson
— 25th Georgia
— 29th Georgia
— 30th Georgia
— 1st Georgia Btn *Sharpshooters*
— 4th Louisiana Battalion

ARMY OF TENNESSEE - CONFEDERATION

Artillery:
— Howell's (Georgia) Battery

Liddell's Division
Brigadier General St. John R. Liddell
Liddell's Bde:
Colonel Daniel C. Govan
— 2nd Arkansas
— 15th Arkansas
— 5th Arkansas
— 13th Arkansas
— 6th Arkansas
— 7th Arkansas
— 8th Arkansas
— 1st Louisiana (Regulars)
Walthall's Bde:
Brigadier General Edward C. Walthall
— 24th Mississippi
— 27th Mississippi
— 29th Mississippi
— 30th Mississippi
— 34th Mississippi
Artillery
Captain Charles Swett
— Fowler's (Alabama) Battery
— Warren Light Artillery *(Mississippi Battery)*

LONGSTREET'S CORPS
Maj. Gen John B. Hood

Hood's Division
Major General John B. Hood
Brigadier General E. McIver Law
Law's Brigade
Brigadier General E. McIver Law
Colonel James L. Sheffield
— 4th Alabama
— 15th Alabama
— 44th Alabama
— 47th Alabama
— 48th Alabama
Robertson's Brigade
Brigadier Gen. Jerome B. Robertson
Colonel Van H; Manning
— 3rd Arkansas
— 1st Texas
— 4th Texas
— 5th Texas
Benning's Brigade
Brigadier General Henry L. Benning
— 2nd Georgia
— 15th Georgia
— 17th Georgia
— 20th Georgia

McLaw's Division
Brig Gen Joseph B. Kershaw

— 2nd South Carolina
— 3rd South Carolina
— 7th South Carolina
— 8th South Carolina
— 15th South Carolina
— 3rd South Carolina Battalion
Humphrey's Brigade
Brigadier Gen. Benjamin G. Humphreys
— 13th Mississippi
— 17th Mississippi
— 18th Mississippi
— 21st Mississippi
Reserve Artillery
Maj Felix Robertson
— Barret's (Missouri) Battery
— Le Gardeur's (Louisiana) Battery
— Havi's (Alabama) Battery
— Massenburg's (Georgia) Battery

LEFT WING
Lieutenant General James Longstreet

Hindman's Division
Major General Thomas C. Hindman
Brigadier General Patton Anderson
Lenoir's Company, Alabama Cavalry escort)
Anderson's Brigade

Brigadier General Patton Anderson
Colonel J. H. Sharp
— 7th Mississippi
— 9th Mississippi
— 10th Mississippi
— 41st Mississippi
— 44th Mississippi
— 9th Mississippi Btn Sharpshooters
— Garrity's (Alabama) Battery
Deas' Brigade
Brigadier General Zach C. Deas
— 19th Alabama
— 22nd Alabama
— 25th Alabama
— 39th Alabama
— 50th Alabama
— 17th Alabama Btn *Sharpshooters*
— Dent's (Alabama) Battery
Manigault's Bde:
Brig Gen Arthur M; Manigault
— 24th Alabama
— 28th Alabama
— 24th Alabama
— 10th South Carolina
— 19th South Carolina
— Water's (Alabama) Battery

Hill's Corps
Lieutenant General Daniel H. Hill

Cleburne's Division
Major General Patrick R. Cleburne
(Sander's Company, Tennessee Cavalry, escort)
Wood's Brigade
Brigadier General S. A. M. Wood
— 16th Alabama
— 33rd Alabama
— 45th Alabama
— 18th Alabama Battalion
— 32nd Mississippi
— 45th Mississippi
— 15th Mississippi Btn *Sharpshooters*
Polk's Brigade
Brig Gen Lucius E. Polk
— 1st Arkansas
— 3rd Confederate Infantry
— 5th Confederate Infantry
— 2nd Tennessee
— 35th Tennessee
Deshler's Brigade
Brigadier General James Deshier
Colonel Roger Q. Mills
— 19th Arkansas
— 24th Arkansas
— 6th Texas Infantry
— 10th Texas Infantry
— 15th Texas Cavalry
— 17th Texas Cavalry
— 18th Texas Cavalry
— 24th Texas Cavalry
— 25th Texas Cavalry
Artillery
Major T. R. Hotchkiss
Captain Henry C. Semple
— Calvert's (Arkansas) Battery
— Douglas' (Texas) Battery
— Semple's (Alabama) Battery

Breckinridge's Division
Maj Gen John C. Breckinridge
(Foule's Company, Mississippi Cavalry escorte)
Helm's Brigade
Brigadier General Benjamin H. Helm
Colonel Joseph H. Lewis
— 41st Alabama
— 2nd Kentucky
— 4th Kentucky
— 6th Kentucky
— 9th Kentucky
Adam's Brigade
Brigadier General Daniel W. Adams
Colonel Randall L. Gibson

— 32nd Alabama
— 13th Louisiana
— 20th Louisiana
— 16th Louisiana
— 25th Louisiana
— 19th Louisiana
— 14th Louisiana Battalion
Stovall's Brigade
Brigadier General Marcellus A. Stovall
— 1st Florida
— 3rd Florida
— 4th Florida
— 47th Georgia
— 60th North Carolina
Artillery
Major Rice E. Graves
— Cobb's (Kentucky) Battery
— Grave's (Kentucky) Battery
— Mebane's 5th Tennessee Battery
— Slocomb's (Louisiana) Battery

BRUCKER'S CORPS
Major General Simon B. Buckner
(Clark's Company, Tennessee Cavalry, escorte)
Reserve Corps Artillery
Major Samuel C. Williams
Baxter's (Tennessee) Battery
Darden's (Mississippi) Battery
Kolb's (Alabama) Battery
McCants' (Florida) Battery

Johnson's Division
Brigadier General Bushrod R. Johnson
Gregg's Brigade
Brig Gen John Gregg
Col Cyrus A. Sugg
— 3rd Tennessee
— 10th Tennessee
— 30th Tennessee
— 41st Tennessee
— 50th Tennessee
— 1st Tennessee Battalion
— 7th Texas Bledsoe's (Missouri) Battery
McNair's Brigade
Brigadier General Evander McNair
Colonel David Coleman
— 1st Arkansas Mounted Rifles
— 2nd Arkansas Mounted Rifles
— 25th Arkansas
— 4th Arkansas
— 31st Arkansas
— 4th Arkansas Battalion
— 39th North Carolina
— Culpepper's (South Carolina) Battery

Preston's Division
Brigadier General William Preston
Gracie's Brigade
Brigadier General Archibald Gracie Jr
— 43rd Alabama
— 1st Alabama Battalion
— 2nd Alabama Battalion
— 3rd Alabama Battalion
— 4th Alabama Battalion
— 63rd Tennessee
Trigg's Brigade
Colonel Robert C. Trigg
— 1st Florida cavalry
— 6th Florida
— 7th Florida
— 54th Virginia
Third Brigade
Colonel John H. Kelly
— 65th Georgia
— 5th Kentucky
— 58th North Carolina
— 63rd Virginia
Artillery Battalion
Major A. Leyden
— Jeffress' (Virginia) Battery
— Peoples' (Georgia) Battery
— Wolihins' (Georgia) Battery

Stewart's Division
Major General Alexander P. Stewart
Johnson's Brigade
Brigadier General Bushrod R. Johnson
Colonel John S. Fulton
— 17th Tennessee
— 23rd Tennessee
— 25th Tennessee
— 44th Tennessee
Bate's Brigade
Brigadier General William B. Bate
— 58th Alabama
— 37th Georgia
— 4th Georgia Btn Sharpshooters
— 15th Tennessee
— 37th Tennessee
— 20th Tennessee
Brown's Brigade
Brigadier General C. Cook
— 18th Tennessee
— 26th Tennessee
— 32nd Tennessee
— 45th Tennessee
— 23rd Tennessee Battalion
Clayton's Brigade
Brigadier General Henry D. Clayton
— 18th Alabama
— 36th Alabama
— 38th Alabama
Artillery
Major J. Wesley Eldridge
— 1st Arkansas Battery
— T. H. Dawson's (Georgia) Battery
— Eudaula Artillery (Alabama) Battery
— Company E, 9th Georgia Artillery Btn.

FORREST'S CORPS
Brigadier General Nathan B. Forrest
(Jackson's Company, Tennessee Cavalry, escorte)

Armstrong's Division
Brigadier General Franck C. Armstrong
Armstrong's Brigade
Colonel James T. Wheeler
— 3rd Arkansas;
— 2nd Kentucky
— 6th Tennessee
— 18th Tennessee
Forrest's Brigade
Colonel George G. Dibrell
— 4th Tennessee
— 8th Tennessee
— 9th Tennessee
— 10th Tennessee
— 11th Tennessee
— Shaw's & O. P. Hamilton's Btn
— R. D. Allison's Squadron
— Huggin's (Tennessee) Battery
— Morton's (Tennessee) Battery

Pegram's Division
Brig Gen John Pegram
Davidson's Brigade
Brigadier General H. B. Davidson
— 1st Georgia
— 6th Georgia
— 6th North Carolina
— Rucker's (1st Tennessee) Legion
— Huwald's (Tennessee) Battery
Scott's Bde:
Colonel John S. Scott
— 10th Confederate Infantry
— John H. Morgan's command *(detachment)*
— 1st Louisiana
— 2nd Tennessee
— 5th Tennessee
— Robinson's (Louisiana) Btty (1 section)

81

BIBLIOGRAPHY

- **The illustrated history of the american soldiers, his uniforms, his equipment**
- **The red legs, US Artillery form 1861 to 1898**
  J. P. Langellier, *Stackpole Books*
- **Echoes of Glories**
  Time Life Books
- **The fighting men of the Civil War.**
  William C. Davis, *Salamander book*
- **Soldier in America.**
  Don Troiani, E.J Coates, J.L Kochan, *Stackpole Books*
- **The american soldier.**
  P. Katcher, R. Volstad, *Osprey Military*
- **American Civil War Union Army**
  R. Smith, C. Collingwood

- **Military images. Photographic History of the US Soldier and sailors in the XIX Century**
  Sandstone Road, Henryville PA
- **US Infantry Equipment**
  P. Katcher et B. Fosten, *Osprey Men at Arms* n° 214
- **Union Cavalryman**
  P. Katcher, R. Hook, *Osprey Warrior serie* n°13
- **Long Knives**
  J. P. Langellier in *Military Illustrated* n°57
- **The Horse Soldier 1776-1943**
  R. Steffen, volume II, *University of Oklahoma Press*
- **Le cavalier nordiste en 1863**
  P. Katcher, (traduction Louis Delpérier) in *Uniformes* n° 95

- *Dakota State University* Web Site

ACKNOWLEDGEMENTS

We should like to thank *Morgan Gillard, Denis Gillé, Sylvaine Noël* for the care that they have taken with the production of this work. *Christophe Caillaux, Dominique Sanches* et *Nicolas Stratigos* for their precious help during the realisation of these books.

Design and lay-out by Jean-Marie MONGIN, © Histoire & Collections 2000
Photographs © Stefan CIEJKA. back cover

All rights reserved. No part of this publication can be transmitted or reproduced without the written consent of the Author and the Publisher.
ISBN : 2 913 903 002
Publisher's number : 2-908182
© Histoire & Collections 2000

A book published by
HISTOIRE & COLLECTIONS
SA au capital de 1 200 000 francs

5, avenue de la République
F-75541 Paris Cédex 11
Phone 01 40 21 18 20
Fax   01 47 00 51 11

This book has been designed, typed, laid-out and processed
by *Histoire & Collections*,
fully on integrated computer equipment.

Printed by KSG-Elkar / KSG-Danona, Spain, European Union.
15 October 2000